MW00587894

Power from On High

or

The Secret of Success in Christian Life and Christian Work

D.L. Moody

'Ye shall receive power'
(Acts 1:8)

Sovereign World

Sovereign World Ltd
PO Box 777
Tonbridge
Kent, TN11 9XT
England

ISBN 1 85240 111 7

Typeset by CRB (Drayton) Typesetting Services, Drayton, Norwich
Printed in England by Clays Ltd, St Ives plc

Preface

One man may have *'zeal without knowledge'*, while another may have knowledge without zeal. If I could have only the one, I believe I should choose the first. But, with an open Bible, no one *need* be without knowledge of God's will and purpose; and the object of this book is to help others to know the source of true **power**, that both their zeal and their knowledge may be of increased service in the Master's work.

Contents

～ ～

'In vain do the inhabitants of London go to their conduits for supply unless the man who has the master-key turns the water on; and in vain do we think to quench our thirst at ordinances, unless God communicates the living water of His Spirit.'   *Anon*

'It was the custom of the Roman emperors, at their triumphal entrance, to cast new coins among the multitudes; so doth Christ, in His triumphal ascension into heaven, throw the greatest gifts for the good of men that were ever given.'   *Thomas Goodwin*

'To unconverted persons, a great part of the Bible resembles a letter written in cipher. The blessed Spirit's office is to act as God's decipherer, by letting His people into the secret of celestial experience, as the key and clue to those sweet mysteries of grace which were before as a garden shut up, or as a fountain sealed, or as a book written in an unknown character.'   *Augustus Toplady*

'The greatest, strongest, mightiest plea for the Church of God in the world is the existence of the Spirit of God in its midst; and the works of the Spirit of God are the true evidences of Christianity. They say miracles are withdrawn; but the Holy Spirit is the standing miracle of the Church of God to-day. I will not say a word against Societies for Christian Evidences, nor against those weighty and learned brethren who have defended the outworks of the Christian Church. They have done good service, and I wish them every blessing; but as to my own soul, I never was settled in my faith in Christ by Paley's 'Evidences,' nor by all the evidence ever brought from history or elsewhere. The Holy Spirit has taken the burden off my shoulders, and given me peace and liberty. This to me is evidence: and as to the externals which we can quote to others, it was enough for Peter and John that the people saw the lame man healed, and they needed not to speak for themselves.'   *C.H. Spurgeon*

～ ～

Chapter 1

Power – Its Source

'Ye shall receive power after that the Holy Ghost is come upon you.'   (Acts 1:8)

'Without the soul divinely quickened and inspired, the observances of the grandest ritualism are as worthless as the motions of a galvanized corpse.' I quote this sentence from an unknown writer, as it leads me at once to the subject under consideration. What is this quickening and inspiration? What is this 'power' needed? Whence its source? I reply: 'The Holy Spirit of God.' I am a full believer in the Apostles' Creed, and therefore 'I believe in the Holy Ghost.'

A writer has pointedly said: 'What are our souls without His grace? – as dead as the branch in which the sap does not circulate. What is the Church without Him? – as parched and barren as the fields without the dew and rain of heaven.'

There has been much inquiry of late on the subject of the Holy Spirit. In this and other lands thousands of persons have been giving attention to the study of this grand theme. I hope it will lead us all to pray for a greater manifestation of His power upon the whole Church of God. How much we have dishonoured Him in the past! How ignorant of His grace, and love, and presence, we have been! True, we have heard of Him and read of Him; but we have had little intelligent knowledge of His attributes, His offices, and His relations to us. I fear He has not been to many professed Christians an actual existence, nor is He known to them as a personality of the Godhead.

7

The first work of the Spirit is to give life – spiritual life. He gives it and He sustains it. If there is no life, there can be no power. As Solomon says: *'A living dog is better than a dead lion.'* When the Spirit imparts this life, He does not leave us to droop and die, but constantly fans the flame. He is ever with us. Surely we ought not to be ignorant of His power and His work.

Identity and Personality

In 1 John 5:7, we read: *'There are three that bear record in heaven, the Father, the Word, and the Holy Ghost; and these three are one.'* By the Father is meant the first Person; Christ, the Word, is the second; and the Holy Spirit, perfectly fulfilling His own office and work in union with the Father and the Son, is the third. I find clearly presented in my Bible, that the One God who demands my love, service, and worship, has there revealed Himself; and that each of those three names of Father, Son, and Holy Ghost, has personality attached to it. Therefore we find some things ascribed to God as Father, some to God as Saviour, and some to God as Comforter and Teacher. It has been remarked that the Father plans, the Son executes, and the Holy Spirit applies. But I also believe they plan and work together.

The distinction of *persons* is often noted in Scripture. In Matthew 3:16, 17, we find **Jesus** submitting to baptism; the **Spirit** descending upon Him; while the **Father's** voice of approval is heard saying: *'This is My Beloved Son, in whom I am well-pleased.'* Again, in John 14:16, we read: *'I* (i.e., Jesus) *will pray the Father, and He shall give you another Comforter.'* Also in Ephesians 2:18: *'Through Him* (i.e., Christ Jesus) *we both* (Jews and Gentiles) *have access by one Spirit unto the Father.'* Thus we are taught the distinction of persons in the Godhead, and their inseparable union. From these and other Scriptures also we learn the identity and actual existence of the Holy Spirit.

If you ask, Do you *understand* what is thus revealed in Scripture? I say, 'No.' But my faith bows down before the inspired Word; and I unhesitatingly believe the great things of God, when even reason is blinded and the intellect confused.

In addition to the teaching of God's Word, the Holy Spirit in His gracious work in the soul declares His own presence. Through His agency we are 'born again'; and through His indwelling we possess superhuman power. Science, falsely so called, when arrayed against the existence and presence of the Spirit of God with His people, only exposes its own folly to those who have become *'new creatures in Christ Jesus.'* The Holy Spirit, who inspired prophets, and qualified apostles, continues to animate, guide, and comfort all true believers. To the actual Christian, the personality of the Holy Spirit is more real than any theory science has to offer; for so-called science is but calculation based on human observation, and is constantly changing its inferences. But the existence of the Holy Spirit is to the child of God a matter of Scripture revelation and of actual experience.

Some sceptics assert that there is no other vital energy in the world but physical force; while contrary to their assertions, thousands and tens of thousands who cannot possibly be deceived have been quickened into spiritual life by a power neither physical nor mental. Men who were dead in sins – drunkards who had lost their will, blasphemers who had lost their purity, libertines sunk in foulness, infidels who published their shame to the world, have in numberless instances become the subjects of the Spirit's power, and are now walking in the true nobility of Christian manhood, separated by an infinite distance from their former life. Let others reject, if they will, at their own peril, this imperishable truth.

I believe, and am growing more into this belief, that divine, miraculous, creative power resides in the Holy Ghost. Above and beyond all natural law, yet in harmony with it, creation, providence, the Divine government, and the upbuilding of the Church of God, are presided over by the Spirit of God. His ministration is the ministration of life, more glorious than the ministration of law (2 Corinthians 3:6–10). And like the Eternal Son, the Eternal Spirit having life in Himself, is working out all things after the counsel of His own will, and for the everlasting glory of the Triune Godhead.

The Holy Spirit has all the qualities belonging to a person; the power to understand, to will, to do, to call, to feel, to love. This cannot be said of a mere 'influence.' He possesses attributes and qualities which can only be ascribed to **A Person**, as acts and deeds are performed by Him which could not be performed by a machine, or by an influence.

The Agent and the Instrument

The Holy Spirit is closely identified with the words of the Lord Jesus.

> *'It is the Spirit that quickeneth; the flesh profiteth nothing: the words that I speak unto you, they are spirit and they are life.'*   (John 6:63)

The Gospel proclamation cannot be divorced from the Holy Spirit. Unless He attend the word in power, vain will be the attempt to preach it. Human eloquence or persuasiveness of speech are the mere trappings of the dead, if the living Spirit be absent. The prophet may preach to the bones in the valley; but it must be the breath from Heaven which will cause the slain to live (Ezekiel 37:9).

In the first epistle of Peter (3:18) we read,

> *'For Christ also hath once suffered for sins, the Just for the unjust, that He might bring us to God, being put to death in the flesh, but quickened by the Spirit.'*

Here we see that Christ was raised up from the grave by this same Spirit; and the power exercised to raise Christ's dead body must raise our dead souls and quicken them. No other power on earth can quicken a dead soul, but the same power that raised the body of Jesus out of Joseph's sepulchre. And if we want that power to quicken our friends who are dead in sin, we must look to God, and not be looking to man, to put it forth. If we look alone to ministers – if we look alone to Christ's disciples – to do this work, we shall be disappointed; but if we look to the Spirit of God and expect the power to come from Him and Him alone, then we shall honour the Spirit, and the Spirit will do His work.

The Secret of Efficiency

I cannot but believe that there are many Christians who want to be more efficient in the Lord's service. The object of this book is to take up this subject of the Holy Spirit, that those who have this desire may see from whom to expect this power. In the teaching of Christ, we find the last words recorded in the Gospel of Matthew 28:19,

> '*Go ye therefore and **teach** all nations, baptizing them in the **name** of the Father, and of the Son, and of the Holy Ghost.*'

Here we find that the Holy Spirit and the Son are equal with the Father – are one with Him:

> '*baptizing them in the name of the Father, and of the Son, and of the Holy Ghost: teaching them to observe all things whatsoever I have commanded you.*'

Christ was now handing His commission over to His apostles. He was going to leave them. His work on earth was finished, and He was now ready to take His seat at the right hand of God.

At this time He spake unto the apostles and said: '*All power is given unto Me in heaven and in earth.*' '*All power.*' So then He had authority. If Christ were mere man, as some people endeavour to make out, it would have been blasphemy for Him to have said to the disciples, Go and baptize all nations in the name of the Father, and in His own name, and in that of the Holy Ghost, making Himself equal with the Father.

There are three things: *All power is given unto Me. Go teach all nations.* Teach them what? *To observe all things.*

11

There are a great many people now who are willing to observe only what they like about Christ; but the things that they do not like they just dismiss and turn away from. But His commission to His disciples was, *'Go teach all nations to observe **all** things whatsoever I have commanded you.'* And what right has a messenger, who has been sent of God, to change the message? If I had sent a servant to deliver a message, and the servant thought the message did not sound exactly right – a little harsh – and that servant went and changed the message, I should change servants very quickly: he would not serve me much longer. And when a minister or a messenger of Christ begins to change the message because he fancies it is not exactly what it ought to be, and thinks he is wiser than God, God just dismisses that man.

Some of the messengers have not taught *'all things'*. They have left out some of the things that Christ has commanded us to teach, because they did not correspond with man's reason. Now we have to take the Word of God just as it is; and if we are going to take it, we have no authority to leave out just what we like – what we think is inappropriate; and let dark reason be our guide.

It is the work of the Spirit to impress the heart and seal the preached word. His office is to take of the things of Christ and reveal them unto us.

Some people have an idea that the present is the only dispensation of the Holy Ghost; that He did not act until Christ was glorified. But of Simeon we read that *'the Holy Ghost was upon him,'* and that it was *'revealed unto him by the Holy Ghost that he should not see death before he had seen the Lord's Christ;'* and when the infant Jesus was brought into the Temple to be presented before the Lord, Simeon also came *'by the Spirit'* into the Temple, and his satisfied soul gave utterance to the words,

> *'Lord, now lettest Thou Thy servant depart in peace, for mine eyes have seen Thy salvation.'*   (Luke 2:25–32)

Returning to our special subject, in 2 Peter 1:21, we read:

> *'Holy men of old spake as they were moved by the Holy Ghost.'*

We find the same Spirit in Genesis as is seen in Revelation. The same Spirit that guided the hand which wrote Exodus inspired also the Epistles; and it is the same Spirit that speaks from one end of the Bible to the other. So holy men in all ages have spoken as they were moved by the Holy Ghost.

His Personality

I was a Christian a long time before I found out that the Holy Ghost was a Person. Now this is something a great many people do not seem to understand; but if you will just take up the Bible and see what Christ had to say about the Holy Spirit, you will find that He always spoke of Him as a Person – that He never spoke of Him as an influence. Some people have an idea that the Holy Spirit is an attribute of God, just like mercy – just an influence coming from God. But we read in John 14:16, these words:

> *'I will pray the Father, and He shall give you another Comforter, that He may abide with you for ever.'*

That *He* may abide with you for ever. And, again, in verse 17:

> *'Even the Spirit of Truth, whom the world cannot receive, because it seeth Him not, neither knoweth Him: but ye know Him; for He dwelleth with you, and shall be in you.'*

Again, in verse 26 of the same chapter:

> *'But the Comforter, which is the Holy Ghost, whom the Father will send in My name, He shall teach you all things, and bring all things to your remembrance, whatsoever I have said unto you.'*

Observe the pronouns 'He' and 'Him.' I want to call attention to this fact – that whenever Christ spoke of the

Holy Ghost He spoke of Him as a Person, not a mere influence; and if we want to honour the Holy Ghost, let us bear in mind that He is one of the Trinity, a personality of the Godhead.

The Reservoir of Love

We read that the first fruit of the Spirit is 'love' (Galatians 5:22). *'God is love;'* Christ is love; and we should not be surprised to read about the *'love of the Spirit'* (Romans 15:30). What a blessed attribute is this! May I call it? – the dome of the temple of the graces. Better still, it is the crown of crowns worn by the Triune God. Human love is a natural emotion which flows forth towards the object of our affections. But Divine love is as high above human love as the heavens are above the earth. The natural man is of the earth, earthy; and however pure his love may be, it is weak and imperfect at best. But the love of God is perfect and entire, wanting nothing. It is as a mighty ocean in its greatness, dwelling with and flowing from the Eternal Spirit.

In Romans 5:5, we read:

> *'And hope maketh not ashamed, because the love of God is shed abroad in our hearts by the Holy Ghost, which is given to us.'*

Now, if we are co-workers with God, there is one thing we must possess, and that is love. A man may be a very successful lawyer and have no love for his clients, and yet get on very well. A man may be a very successful physician and have no love for his patients, and yet be a very good physician. A man may be a very successful merchant and have no love for his customers, and yet he may do a good business and succeed. But no man can be a co-worker with God without love. If our service is mere profession on our part, the quicker we renounce it the better. If a man takes up God's work as he would take up any profession, the sooner he gets out of it the better.

We cannot work for God without love. It is the only tree

14

on this sin-cursed earth that can produce fruit that is acceptable to God. If I have no love for God nor for my fellowman, then I cannot work acceptably. I am like sounding brass and a tinkling cymbal. As I pointed out just now, we are told that *'the love of God is shed abroad in our hearts by the Holy Ghost.'* Now, if we have had that love shed abroad in our hearts, we are ready for God's service; if we have not, we are not ready. It is so easy to reach a man when you love him; all barriers are broken down and swept away.

Paul, when writing to Titus (2:2), tells him that the aged men are to be *'sound in faith, in charity, and in patience.'* Now, in this age, ever since I can remember, the Church has been very jealous about men being unsound in the faith. If a man becomes unsound in the faith, they draw their ecclesiastical sword and cut at him; but he may be ever so unsound in love, and they say nothing. He may be ever so defective in patience; he may be irritable and fretful all the time; but they never deal with him.

Now, the Bible teaches us, that we are not only to be sound in the faith, but in charity, and in patience. I believe God cannot use many of His servants, because they are full of irritability and impatience; they are fretting all the time, from morning until night. God cannot use them; their mouths are sealed; they cannot speak for Jesus Christ. If they have not love, they cannot work for God. I do not mean love for those who love me; it does not require grace to feel that; the rudest pagan in the world can feel that; the greatest heathen that ever lived can feel that; the vilest man that ever walked the earth can feel that. That does not require any grace at all. I did that before I ever became a Christian.

Love begets love; hatred begets hatred. If I know a man loves me first I know my love will be going out towards him. Suppose a man comes to me, saying, 'Mr Moody, a certain man told me to-day that he thought you were the meanest man living.' Well, if I had not a good deal of the grace of God in my heart, then I know that hard feelings would spring up in my heart against that man, and it would not be long before I would be talking against him. Hatred begets hatred.

Suppose, however, a man comes to me and says, 'Mr Moody, do you know that such a man whom I met to-day says that he thinks a great deal of you?' Though I may never have heard of him, love would be at once springing up in my heart. Love begets love – we all know that; but it takes the grace of God to make me love the man who tells lies about me, the man who slanders me, the man who is trying to damage my character; it requires the grace of God to enable me to love that man. You may hate the sin he has committed; there is a difference between the sin and the sinner; you may hate the one with a perfect hatred, but you must love the sinner. Otherwise you cannot do him any good.

You know the first impulse of a young convert is to love. Do you remember the day on which you were converted? Was not your heart full of sweet peace and love?

The Right Overflow

I remember the morning on which I came out of my room after I had first trusted Christ. I thought the old sun shone a good deal brighter than it ever had before; I thought that the sun was just smiling upon me; and I walked out upon Boston Common, and heard the birds singing in the trees, and I thought they were all singing a song for me. Do you know – I fell in love with the birds. I had never cared for them before. It seemed to me that I was in love with all creation. I had not a bitter feeling against any man, and I was ready to take all men to my heart.

If a man has not the love of God shed abroad in his heart, he has never been regenerated. If you hear a person get up in the prayer-meeting, and he begins to find fault with everybody, you may doubt whether his is a genuine conversion; it may be counterfeit; it has not the right ring; because the impulse of a converted soul is to love, and not to be getting up and complaining of everyone else, and finding fault.

But it is hard for us to live in the right atmosphere all the time. Someone comes along and treats us wrongly. Perhaps, as a consequence, we hate him. We have not attended to the means of grace, nor kept feeding on the Word of God, as we ought; a root of bitterness springs up in our hearts, although we may hardly be aware of it: then we are not qualified to work for God; the love of God is *not* shed abroad in our hearts, as it ought to be, by the Holy Ghost.

But the work of the Holy Ghost is to impart love. Paul could say, *'The love of Christ constraineth us'* (2 Corinthians 5:14). He could not help going from city to city and preaching the Gospel. Jeremiah at one time said, *'I will not speak any more in the Lord's name'* (20:9); as though he would say, 'I have suffered enough; these people do not like God's word.' He lived in a wicked day, as we do now. Infidels were creeping up all around him, who said the word of God was not true; Jeremiah had stood like a wall of fire, confronting them, and he boldly proclaimed that the word of God was true. At last they put him in prison, and he seemed to think, 'I will keep still; it has cost me too much.' But a little while after, you know, he *could not* keep still. His bones caught fire; he had to speak. And when we are so full of the love of God that we are compelled to work for God, *then* God blesses us. If our work is only done by compulsion, without any true motive power, it will come to nought.

Now the question comes up, Have we the love of God shed abroad in our hearts? and are we speaking the truth in love? Some people speak the truth, but in such a cold stern way that it will do no good. Other people want to love everything, and so they give up much of the truth. But we are to speak the truth in love; we are to speak the truth even if we lose all; but we are to speak it in love, and if we do that, the Lord will bless us.

There are a good many people trying to get this love; they are trying to produce it of themselves. But therein all fail. The love implanted deep in our new nature will be spontaneous. I have not to learn to love my children. I cannot help loving them. A young miss some time ago, in an inquiry meeting, said that she could not love God; that it was very hard for her to love Him. I said to her, 'Is it hard for you to love your mother? Do you have to learn to love your mother?' And she looked up through her tears, and said, 'No, I cannot help doing so, that is spontaneous.' 'Well,' I said, 'when the Holy Spirit kindles love in your heart, you cannot help loving God; it will be spontaneous.' When the Spirit of God comes into your heart and mine, it will be easy to serve God.

The fruit of the Spirit, as you find it in Galatians, begins with 'love.' There are nine graces spoken of in the fifth chapter, and of the nine different graces Paul puts 'love' at the head of the list; **Love** is the first thing – the first in that precious cluster of fruit. Someone has put it in this way: that all the other eight can be included in the word – love. **Joy** is love exulting; **peace** is love in repose; **long-suffering** is love on trial; **gentleness** is love outflowing; **goodness** is love in action; **faith** is love on the battlefield; **meekness** is love at school; and **temperance** is love in training.

So it is **love** all the way; love at the top; love at the bottom, and all the way along through these graces. And if every one just brought forth the fruit of the Spirit, what a world we should have! There would be no need of any policemen; a man could leave his overcoat about without someone stealing it; men would have no desire to do evil. Speaking of these nine Christian graces Paul says, *'Against such there is no law.'* You need no law. A man who is full of the Spirit does not require to be put under law; does not need any policeman to watch him. We could dismiss all our policemen; the lawyers would have to give up practising law; and the courts would have no business.

The Triumphs of Hope

In Romans 15:13, the Apostle says:

> *'Now the God of hope fill you with all joy and peace in believing, that ye may abound in hope, through the power of the Holy Ghost.'*

The next thing then is **Hope**.

Did you ever notice this – that no man or woman who has lost hope is ever used by God to build up His kingdom? Now, I have been observing this throughout different parts of the country; and wherever I have found a worker in God's vineyard who has lost hope, I have found a man or woman who is not very useful. Now, just look at these workers. Let your mind go over the past for a moment. Can you think of a man or woman whom God has used to build His kingdom, who has lost hope? I know of none; I never heard of such a one. It is very important to have **hope** in the Church; and it is the work of the Holy Ghost to impart hope. Let Him come into some of the churches where there have been no conversions for a few years, and let Him convert a score of people, and see how hopeful the Church becomes at once. God's Spirit imparts hope. A man filled with the Spirit of God will be very hopeful: he will be looking out into the future, and he knows that it is all bright, because the God of all grace is able to do great things. So it is very important that we have hope.

If a man has lost hope, he is out of communion with God; he has not the Spirit of God resting upon him for service; he may be a 'son' of God, and yet so disheartened that he cannot be used of God. Do you know there is no place in the Scriptures where it is recorded that God ever used even a discouraged man.

Some years ago, I was quite discouraged in my work, and was ready to hang my harp upon the willow. I was very much cast down and depressed. I had been for weeks in that state, when one Monday morning a friend, who had a very large Bible class, came into my study. I used to examine the notes of his Sunday-school lessons, which were equal to a sermon, and he came to me this morning, and said, 'Well, what did you preach about yesterday?' and I told him. I said, 'What did you preach about?' and he said that he preached about Noah. 'Did you ever preach about Noah?' said he. 'No, I never preached about Noah.' 'Did you ever study his character.' 'No, I never studied his life particularly.' 'Well,' says he, 'he is a most wonderful character. It will do you good to consider it. You ought to study that character.'

When he went out, I took down my Bible and read about Noah; and then it came over me that Noah worked a hundred and twenty years and never made a convert; and yet he did not get discouraged. Then said I, 'Well, I ought not to be discouraged,' and I closed my Bible, got up, and walked down town; and the cloud had gone. I went down to the noon prayer-meeting, and heard of a little town in the country where they had taken into the church a hundred young converts; and I said to myself, 'I wonder what Noah would have given if he could have heard that;' and yet he worked a hundred and twenty years and did not get discouraged. And then a man right across the aisle got up and said: 'My friends, I wish you to pray for me; I think I am lost;' and I thought to myself, 'I wonder what Noah would have given to hear that.' He never heard a man say, 'I wish you to pray for me; I think I am lost;' and yet he did not get discouraged!

Oh, children of God, let us not get discouraged; let us ask God to forgive us, if we have been discouraged and cast down; let us ask God to give us 'hope', that we may be ever hopeful. It does me good sometimes to meet some people and take hold of their hands – they are so hopeful; while other people throw a gloom over me because they are all the time cast down, and looking at the dark side, contemplating the obstacles and difficulties in the way.

The Boon of Liberty

Another thing the Spirit of God gives us is **liberty** (Galatians 5:1). He first imparts *love*; He next inspires *hope*; and then gives *liberty* – and that is about the last thing we have in a good many of our churches at the present day. And I am sorry to say there must be a funeral in a good many churches before there is much work done; we shall have to bury the formalism so deep that it will never have any resurrection. The last thing to be found in many a church is liberty.

If the Gospel happens to be preached, the people criticise as they would a theatrical performance. It is exactly the same; and many a professed Christian never thinks of listening to what the man of God has to say. It is hard work to preach to carnally-minded critics; but *'where the Spirit of the Lord is, there is liberty.'*

Very often someone will hear a hundred good things in a

sermon; and there may be one thing that strikes them as a little out of place: they will go home and sit down at the table, and talk right out before the children, magnifying that one wrong thing, and not saying a word about the hundred good things that were uttered. That is what people who criticise do.

God does not use men in captivity. The condition of many is like that of Lazarus when he came out of the sepulchre bound hand and foot. The bandage was not taken off his mouth, and he could not speak. He had life – if you had said Lazarus was not alive, you would have told a falsehood, because he was raised from the dead. There are a great many people who, the moment you talk to them and insinuate they are not doing what they might do, say: 'I have life: I am a Christian.' Well, you cannot deny it; but they are bound hand and foot.

May God snap these fetters, and set His children free, that they may have liberty! I believe He desires to set us free, and wants us to work for Him, and speak for Him. How many people would like to get up in a social prayer-meeting to say a few words for Christ! But there is such a cold spirit of criticism in the Church that they dare not do it. They have not the 'liberty' to do it. If they get up they are so frightened at these critics that they begin to tremble and sit down. They cannot say anything. Now, that is all wrong. The Spirit of God comes just to give liberty (Isaiah 61:1), and wherever you see the Lord's work going on, you will see that spirit of liberty. People will not be afraid of speaking to one another. And when the meeting is over they will not get their hats and see how quick they can get out of the church, but will begin to shake hands with one another; and there will be *liberty* there. A good many go to the prayer-meeting out of a mere cold sense of duty. They think, 'I must attend, because I feel it is my duty.' They do not think it is a glorious privilege to meet and pray, and to be strengthened, and to help someone else in the wilderness journey.

What we need to-day is **love** in our hearts. Do we not want it? Do we not want **hope** in our lives? Do we not want to be hopeful? Do we not want **liberty**? Now, all this is the work of

the Spirit of God. Let us pray God daily to give us love, and
hope, and liberty. We read in the Epistle to the Hebrews
(10:19),

*'Having therefore, brethren, boldness to enter into the
holiest by the blood of Jesus.'*

If you will turn to the passage and read the margin – it says:
'Having therefore, brethren, liberty to enter into the holiest.' Having freedom of access, we can go into the holiest,
and plead for this love, and liberty, and glorious hope – that
we may not rest until God gives us the power to work for
Him.

If I know my own heart to-day, I would rather die than live
as I once did, a mere nominal Christian, and not used by
God in building up His kingdom. To live for the sake of self
seems a poor empty life.

Let us seek to be useful. Let us seek to be 'vessels meet for
the Master's use,' that God, the Holy Spirit, may shine fully
through us.

'Know, my soul, thy full salvation;
    Rise o'er sin, and fear, and care;
Joy to find, in every station,
    Something still to do or bear.

'Think what Spirit dwells within thee;
    Think what Father's smiles are thine;
Think that Jesus died to win thee:
    Child of heaven, canst thou repine?

'Haste thee on from grace to glory,
    Armed by faith, and winged by prayer,
Heaven's eternal day's before thee:
    God's own hand shall guide thee there.

'Soon shall close thy earthly mission,
    Soon shall pass thy pilgrim days,
Hope shall change to glad fruition,
    Faith to sight, and prayer to praise.'

❦   ❧

'You remember that strange, half-involuntary "forty years" of Moses in the "wilderness" of Midian, when he had fled from Egypt. You remember, too, the almost equally strange years of retirement in "Arabia" by Paul, when, if ever, humanly speaking, instant action was needed. And pre-eminently you remember the amazing charge of the ascending Lord to the disciples, *"Tarry at Jerusalem."* Speaking after the manner of men, one could not have wondered if out-spoken Peter, or fervid James, had said: "Tarry, Lord! How long?" "Tarry, Lord! is there not a perishing world, groaning for the 'good news'? "Tarry! did we hear Thee aright, Lord? Was the word not? – Haste!" Nay; *"Being assembled together with them, He commanded them that they should not depart from Jerusalem, but wait for the promise of the Father"'* (Acts 1:4).

Grosart

❦   ❧

Chapter 2

Power – 'In' and 'Upon'

The Holy Spirit dwelling in us, is one thing; I think this is clearly brought out in Scripture: and the Holy Spirit upon us for service, is another thing. Now in Scripture we only read of three places that are dwelling-places for the Holy Ghost.

In the 40th chapter of Exodus, commencing with the 33rd verse, are these words:

> '*And he* (that is, Moses) *reared up the court round about the Tabernacle and the altar, and set up the hanging of the court gate. So Moses finished the work. Then a cloud covered the tent of the congregation, and the glory of the Lord filled the Tabernacle. And Moses was not able to enter into the tent of the congregation, because the cloud abode thereon, and the glory of the Lord filled the Tabernacle.*'

The moment that Moses finished the work, the instant that the Tabernacle was ready, the cloud came, the Shekinah glory came, and filled the Tabernacle, so that Moses was not able to stand before the presence of the Lord. I believe firmly, that the moment our hearts are emptied of pride and selfishness, ambition and self-seeking, and everything that is contrary to God's law, the Holy Ghost will come and fill every corner of our hearts. But if we are full of pride and conceit, ambition and self-seeking, pleasure and the world, there is no room for the Spirit of God; and I doubt not many a man is praying to God to fill him, when he is full already with something else. Before we pray that God would fill us, I believe we ought to pray Him to empty us.

There must be an emptying before there can be a filling. When the heart is turned upside down, and everything that is contrary to God turned out, then the Spirit will come, just as He did in the Tabernacle, and fill us with His glory. We read in 2 Chronicles, 5:13:

> *'It came even to pass, as the trumpeters and singers were as one, to make one sound to be heard in praising and thanking the Lord; and when they lifted up their voice with the trumpets and cymbals and instruments of music, and praised the Lord, saying, "For He is good; for His mercy endureth for ever;" that then the house was filled with a cloud, even the house of the Lord; so that the priests could not stand to minister by reason of the cloud, for the glory of the Lord had filled the house of God.'*

Praising with One Heart

We find, the very moment that Solomon completed the Temple, when all was finished, those present were just praising God with one heart: the choristers and the singers and the ministers were all one; there was no discord; they were all praising God. And the glory of God came and just filled the Temple, as it had the Tabernacle. Now, as you pass on to the New Testament, you will find that, instead of the Spirit coming to Tabernacles or Temples, believers are now the Temple of the Holy Ghost. On the day of Pentecost, before Peter preached that memorable sermon, as the disciples were praying, the Holy Ghost came, and came in mighty power. We now pray for the Spirit of God to come, and we sing:

> 'Come, Holy Spirit, heavenly Dove,
>   With all Thy quickening powers;
> Kindle a flame of heavenly love
>   In these cold hearts of ours!'

I believe, if we understand it properly, this prayer is perfectly right. But if we are praying for the Holy Spirit to come out of heaven down to earth again, that is wrong; *because He is already here.* He has not been absent from this earth for eighteen hundred years; He has been in the Church, and He is in all believers. The believers in the Church are the called-out ones; they are called out from the world; and every true believer is a Temple for the Holy Ghost to dwell in. In John we have the words of Jesus:

> *'The Spirit of Truth, whom the world cannot receive, because it seeth Him not, neither knoweth Him; but ye know Him, for He dwelleth with you, and shall be **in you**.'*

*'Greater is He that is **in you** than he that is in the world'* (1 John 4:4). If we have the Spirit dwelling in us, He gives us power over the flesh and the world, and over every enemy. *'He dwelleth with you, and **shall be in you**.'*

Read 1 Corinthians 3:16:

> *'Know ye not that ye are the temple of God, and that the Spirit of God dwelleth in you?'*

There were some men burying an aged saint some time ago. He had been very poor, like many of God's people, poor in this world – but they are very rich, they have all the riches on the other side of life; they have them laid up there where thieves cannot get them, where sharpers cannot take them away, and where moth cannot corrupt; so this aged man was very rich in the other world – and they were just hastening him off to the grave, wanting to get rid of him, when an old minister, who was officiating at the grave, said, 'Tread softly, for you are carrying the temple of the Holy Ghost.' Whenever you see a believer, you see a temple of the Holy Ghost.

In 1 Corinthians 6:19, 20, we read again:

27

> *'Know ye not that your body is the temple of the Holy Ghost, which is in you, which ye have of God? And ye are not your own, for ye are bought with a price; therefore glorify God in your body and in your spirit, which are God's.'*

Thus are we taught that there is a Divine resident in every child of God.

I think it is clearly shown in the Scripture that every believer has the Holy Ghost dwelling in him. He may be quenching the Spirit of God, or he may not glorify God as he should; but if he is a believer on the Lord Jesus Christ, the Holy Ghost dwells in him. But I want to call your attention to another fact. I believe to-day, that though Christian men and women have the Holy Spirit dwelling in them, yet He is not dwelling within them in power; in others words, God has a great many sons and daughters without power.

What is Needed

Nine-tenths, at least, of the church members never think of speaking for Christ. If they see a man, perhaps a near relative, just going right down to ruin, going rapidly, they never think of speaking to him about his sinful course, nor of seeking to win him to Christ. Now certainly there must be something wrong. And yet when you talk with them you find they have faith, and you cannot say they are not children of God; but they have not the 'power,' they have not the 'liberty,' they have not the 'love,' that real disciples of Christ should have.

A great many people are thinking that we need new measures, that we need new churches, that we need new organs, and that we need new choirs, and all these new things. That is not what the Church of God needs to-day. It is *the old power* that the Apostles had, which we want; and if we have that in our churches, there will be new life. Then we shall have new ministers – the same old ministers renewed with power; filled with the Spirit. I remember that in Chicago many were toiling in the work, and it seemed as though the car of salvation did not move on, when a minister began to cry out from the very depths of his heart, 'O God, put new ministers in every pulpit.' On the following Monday I heard two or three men stand up and say, 'We had a new minister last Sunday – the same old minister, but he had got new power,' and I firmly believe that is what we want to-day all over America and England. We want new ministers in the pulpit and new people in the pews. We want people quickened by the Spirit of God, and the Spirit coming down and taking possession of the children of God and giving them power.

Then, a man filled with the Spirit will know how to use the 'sword of the Spirit.' If a man is not filled with the Spirit, he will never know how to use the Bible. We are told that this is the 'sword of the Spirit.' And what is an army good for that does not know how to use its weapons? Suppose a battle was going on, and I were a general, and had a hundred thousand men – great, able-bodied men, full of life – but not one of whom could handle a sword, nor knew how to use his rifle, what would that army be good for? Why, one thousand well-drilled men, with good weapons, would rout the whole of them.

The reason why the Church cannot overcome the enemy is, because she does not know how to use the 'sword of the Spirit.' People will get up and try to fight the devil with their experiences; but he does not care for that; he will overcome them every time. People are trying to fight the devil with theories and pet ideas; but he will get the victory over them likewise. What we want is to draw the 'sword of the Spirit.' It is that which cuts deeper than anything else.

Turn in your Bibles to Ephesians 6:14–17:

> *'Stand therefore, having your loins girt about with truth, and having on the breastplate of righteousness; and your feet shod with the preparation of the gospel of peace: above all* [or over all], *taking the shield of faith, wherewith ye shall be able to quench all the fiery darts of the wicked. And take the helmet of salvation; and the sword of the Spirit, which is the Word of God.'*

The Greatest Weapon

The sword of the Spirit is the Word of God; and what we specially need is to be filled with the Spirit, so that we shall know how to use the Word. A Christian man was talking to a sceptic, and was quoting the Word; the sceptic said, 'I don't believe, sir, in that book.' But the man went right on, and gave him more of the Word; and the sceptic again remarked, 'I don't believe the Bible,' but the Christian kept giving him more; and at last the man was reached. And the brother added, 'When I have proved a good sword, which does execution, I would just keep right on using it.' That is what we want.

Sceptics and infidels may say they do not believe in the Bible. It is not our work to make them believe in it; that is the work of the Spirit. Our work is to give them the Word of God; not to preach our theories and our ideas about it, but just to deliver the message as God gives it to us. We read in the Scriptures of the sword of the Lord and of Gideon. Suppose Gideon had gone out without the Lord's command, he would have been defeated. But the Lord used Gideon; and I think you find all through the Scriptures, that God takes up and uses human instruments. I believe you cannot find in the Bible a case of a man being converted without God calling in some human agency – using some human instrument; not that He could not do it in His independent sovereignty; there is no doubt about that. Even when by the revealed glory of the Lord Jesus, Saul of Tarsus was smitten to the earth, Ananias was used to open his eyes and lead him into the light of the Gospel. I heard a man once say, If you put a man on a mountain peak, higher than one of the Alpine summits, God could save him without a human messenger; but that is not His way; that is not His method; it is *the sword of the Lord and of Gideon*'; and the Lord and Gideon will do the work; and if we are just willing to let the Lord use us, He will.

'None of Self'

Then all through the Scriptures you will find, that when men were filled with the Holy Spirit, they preached Christ, and not themselves. They preached Christ and Him crucified. We read in the first chapter of Luke, 67–70, speaking of Zacharias, the father of John the Baptist:

> *'And his father, Zacharias, was filled with the Holy Ghost, and prophesied, saying: Blessed be the Lord God of Israel, for He hath visited and redeemed His people, and hath raised up an horn of salvation for us in the house of His servant David; as He spake by the mouth of His holy prophets, which have been since the world began.'*

See, he is talking about the Word. If a man is filled with the Spirit, he will magnify the Word; he will preach the Word, and not himself; he will give this lost world the Word of the living God.

> *'And thou, child, shalt be called the prophet of the Highest; for thou shalt go before the face of the Lord to prepare His ways; to give knowledge of salvation unto His people by the remission of their sins, through the tender mercy of our God, whereby the day-spring from on high hath visited us; to give light to them that sit in darkness and in the shadow of death; to guide our feet into the way of peace. And the child grew and waxed strong in spirit, and was in the deserts till the day of his showing unto Israel.'* (Luke 1:76–80)

And so we find again that when Elisabeth and Mary met, they talked of the Scriptures, and they were both filled with the Holy Ghost, and at once began to speak of their Lord.

We also find that Simeon, as he came into the temple and found the young child Jesus there, at once began to quote the Scriptures, for the Spirit was upon him. And when Peter stood up on the day of Pentecost, and preached that wonderful sermon, it is said he was filled with the Holy Ghost, and began to preach the Word to the multitude, and it was the Word that cut them. It was the sword of the Lord and Peter,

the same as it was the sword of the Lord and Gideon. And
we read of Stephen,

> *'They were not able to resist the wisdom and the spirit by
> which he spake.'*   (Acts 6:10)

Why? Because he gave them the Word of God. And we are
told that the Holy Ghost came on Stephen, and none could
resist his word. And we read, too, that Paul was full of the
Holy Spirit; and that he preached Christ and Him crucified,
and many people were added to the Church. Barnabas was
full of the Holy Ghost and of faith (Acts 11:24); and if you
will just read and find out what he preached, you will find it
was the Word; and many were added to the Lord. So that
when a man is full of the Spirit, he begins to preach, not
himself, but Christ, as revealed in the Holy Scriptures.

The disciples of Jesus were all filled with the Spirit, and
the Word was published abroad. And when the Spirit of God
comes down upon the Church, and we are anointed, the
Word will be published in the streets, in the lanes, and in the
alleys; there will not be a dark cellar nor a dark attic, nor a
home, where the Gospel will not be carried by some loving
heart, if the Spirit comes upon God's people in demonstration and in power.

Spiritual Irrigation

It is possible a man may just barely have life, and be satisfied: I think that a great many are in that condition. In the
3rd chapter of John we find that Nicodemus came to Christ,
and that he received life. At first this life was feeble. You do
not hear of him standing up confessing Christ boldly, nor of
the Spirit coming upon him in great power; though he possessed life through faith in Christ. Then turn to the 4th
chapter of John, and you will find it tells of the woman
coming to the well of Samaria; and Christ held out the cup of
salvation to her, and she took it and drank, and it became in
her *'a well of water springing up into everlasting life.'* That is
a better instance of spiritual quickening than we have in the

3rd chapter of John; here salvation came down in a flood into the soul of the Samaritan woman; as someone has said, it came down from the throne of God, and like a mighty current carried her back to the throne of God. Water always rises to its level; and if we get the soul filled with water from the throne of God it will bear us upward to its source.

But if you want to get the best class of Christian life portrayed, turn to the 7th chapter: there you will find it said that he that receiveth the Spirit, through trusting in the Lord Jesus, out of him *'shall flow rivers of living water'* (7:38). Now there are two ways of digging a well. I remember, when a boy, upon a farm in New England, they had a well, and they put in an old wooden pump, and I used to have to pump the water from that well upon washing-day, and to water the cattle; and many a time I had to pump, and pump, and pump, until my arms got tired. But they have a better way now; they do not dig down a few feet and brick up the hole and put the pump in, but they go down through the clay, and the sand, and the rock, and on down until they strike what they call a lower stream, and then the boring becomes an artesian well, which needs no labour, as the water rises spontaneously from the depths beneath.

Now, I think God wants all His children to be something like an artesian well; not to need continual pumping, but having grace flow right out. Why, have you not seen ministers in the pulpit just pumping, and pumping, and pumping? I have, many a time; and I have had to do it, too. I know how it is. They stand in the pulpit, and talk, and talk, and talk, and the people go to sleep; they cannot arouse them. What is the difficulty? Why, the living water is not there; they are just pumping when there is no water in the well. You cannot get water out of a dry well; there must be something in the well, or you cannot get anything out. I have seen those wooden pumps into which you had to pour water before you could pump any water out: and so it is with a good many people; you have to get something into them before you can get anything out. People wonder why it is that they have no spiritual power. They stand up and talk in the meeting, and do not say anything; they say they have nothing to say, and you find that out soon enough; they need not have stated it. They just talk, because they feel it is a duty; and yet they say nothing.

Now, I tell you, when the Spirit of God is on us for service, resting upon us, we are *anointed*; and then we can do great things. *'I will pour water upon him that is thirsty,'* says God (Isaiah 44:3). Oh, blessed thought – *'He that hungers and thirsts after righteousness shall be filled!'*

Outflowing Streams

I should like to see someone just full of 'living water'; so full that he could not contain it; so full that he would have to go out and publish the Gospel of the grace of God. When a man gets so full that he cannot hold any more, then he is just ready for God's service.

When preaching in Chicago, Dr Gibson remarked in the inquiry meeting, 'Now, how can we find out who is thirsty?' Said he, 'I was just thinking how we could find out. If a boy should come down the aisle, bringing a good pailful of clear water, and a dipper, we should soon find out who was thirsty; we should see thirsty men and women reach out for water; but if you were to walk down the aisle with an empty bucket, you would not find out the thirsty ones. People would look in and see that there was no water, and would say nothing. So,' said he, 'I think that is the reason we are not more blessed in our ministry; we are carrying around empty buckets, and the people see that we have nothing in them, and they do not come forward.'

I think that there is a good deal of truth in that. People see that we are carrying around empty buckets, and they will not come to us until they are filled. They see we have no more than they have. We must have the Spirit of God resting upon us; and then we shall have something that gives the victory over the world, the flesh, and the devil; something that gives the victory over our tempers, over our conceits, and over every other evil; and when we can trample these sins under our feet, then people will come to us and say, 'How did you get it? I need this power. You have something that I have not; I want it.' Oh, may God show us this truth! Have we been toiling all night? Let us throw the net on the right side; let us ask God to forgive our sins, and anoint us with power from on high. But remember, He is not going to give this power to an impatient man; He is not going to give it to a selfish man; He will never give it to an ambitious man whose aim is selfish, until he is first emptied of self – emptied of pride and of all worldly thoughts. Let it be God's glory and not our own that we seek; and when we get to that point, how speedily the Lord will bless us for good! Then will the measure of our blessing be full. Do you know what heaven's measure is? *'Good measure, pressed down, shaken together, and running over'* (Luke 6:38).

If we get our heart filled with the Word of God, how is Satan going to get in? how is the world going to get in? – for heaven's measure is good measure, full measure, running over. Have you this fullness? If you have not, then seek it; say by the grace of God you will have it; for it is *'the Father's good pleasure'* to give us these things. He wants us to shine down in this world; He wants to lift us up for His work; He wants us to have the power to testify for His Son. He has left us in this world to testify for Him. What did He leave us for? Not to buy and sell and get gain, but to glorify Christ. How are you going to do it without the Spirit? That is the question. How are you to do it without the power of God?

Why Some Fail

We read in John 20:22:

> *'And when He had said this, He breathed on them, and saith unto them, Receive ye the Holy Ghost.'*

Then see Luke 24:49:

> *'Behold, I send the promise of my Father upon you; but tarry ye in the city of Jerusalem until ye be endued with power from on high.'*

The first passage tells us He had raised those pierced and wounded hands over them, and breathed upon them, and said, *'Receive ye the Holy Ghost.'* And I have not a doubt they received it then; but not in such mighty power as afterwards, when qualified for their work. It was not in fullness that He gave the Spirit to them then; but if they had been like a good many now, they would have said, 'We have enough now; we are not going to tarry; we are going to work.'

Some people seem to think they are losing time if they wait on God for His power; and so away they go and work, without unction; they are working without any anointing; they are working without any power. But after Jesus had said, 'Receive ye the Holy Ghost,' and had breathed on the disciples, He said:

> *'Tarry ye in the city of Jerusalem until ye be endued with power from on high.'*

Read in Acts 1:8:

> *'But ye shall receive power, after that the Holy Ghost is come upon you.'*

Now, the Spirit had certainly been given them, or they could not have believed; and they could not have taken their stand for God and gone through what they did, or endured the scoffs and frowns of their friends, if they had not been converted by the power of the Holy Ghost. But now just see what Christ said:

> *'Ye shall receive power, after that the Holy Ghost is come upon you; and ye shall be witnesses unto Me both in Jerusalem and in all Judea, and in Samaria, and unto the uttermost part of the earth.'*   (Acts 1:8)

Then the Holy Spirit IN us is one thing, and the Holy Spirit ON us is another. And if these Christians had gone out and went right to preaching then and there, without the power, do you think that scene would have taken place on the day of Pentecost? Do you not think that Peter would have stood up there and beat against the air, while those Jews would have gnashed their teeth and mocked him?

But they tarried in Jerusalem; they waited ten days. 'What!' you say: 'what! the world perishing, and men dying! Shall I wait?' Do what God tells you. There is no use in running before you are sent; there is no use in attempting to do God's work without God's power. A man working without this unction; a man working without this anointing; a man working without the Holy Ghost upon him – is losing his time after all. So we are not going to lose anything if we tarry till we get this power. That is the object of true service – to wait on God, to tarry till we receive this power for witness-bearing. Then we find that on the day of Pentecost, ten days after Jesus Christ was glorified, the Holy Spirit descended in power. Do you think that Peter and James and John and those apostles ever, from that very hour, doubted their having received that baptism of the Spirit? They never doubted it.

Perhaps some question the possibility of having the power of God now; and believe that the Holy Spirit never came afterward in similar manifestation, and will never come again in such power.

Fresh Supplies

Turn to Acts 4:31, and you will find the Holy Spirit came a second time, and the place where the disciples were assembled was shaken, and they were filled with this 'power'.

The fact is, we are leaky vessels, and we have to keep right under the fountain all the time to keep full of Christ, and so have a fresh supply. I believe the mistake a great many of us are making is – we are trying to do God's work with the grace God gave us ten years ago. We say, if it is necessary, we will go on with the same grace. Now, what we want is a fresh supply, a fresh anointing and fresh power; and if we seek it, and seek it with all our hearts, we shall obtain it. The early converts were taught to look for that power. Philip went to Samaria, and news reached Jerusalem that there was a great work being done in Samaria, and many converts; and John and Peter went down, and they laid their hands on the new disciples, and they received the Holy Ghost for service (Acts 8). I think that is what we Christians ought to be looking for – the Spirit of God for service – that God may use us mightily in the building up of His Church and hastening His glory.

In Acts 19 we read of twelve men at Ephesus, who, when the inquiry was made if they had received the Holy Ghost since they believed, answered: *'We have not so much as heard whether there be any Holy Ghost.'* I venture to say there are very many, who, if you were to ask them, 'Have you received the Holy Ghost since you believed?' would reply, 'I don't know what you mean by that.' They would be like those twelve men at Ephesus, who had never under- stood the peculiar relation of the Spirit to the children of God in this dispensation. I firmly believe that the Church has just laid this knowledge aside, mislaid it somewhere; and so Christians are without power. Sometimes you can take one hundred fresh members into a Church, and they do not add to its power. Now that is all wrong. If they were only anointed by the Spirit of God, there would be great power if one hundred saved ones were added to the Church.

Green Fields

When I was out in California, the first time I went down from the Sierra Nevada Mountains and descended into the Valley of the Sacramento, I was surprised to find that everything on one farm was green and fertile – all the trees and flowers were blooming, and everything was fresh and beautiful; whilst just across the hedge everything was dried up, and there was not a green thing to be seen. I could not under- stand this: I made inquiries, and I found that the man who had everything green, irrigated; he just poured the water right on the ground, and thus kept everything green, while the fields that were next to his were as dry as Gideon's fleece without a drop of dew; and so it is with a great many in the

Church to-day. They are like these farms in California – a dreary desert, everything parched and desolate, and apparently with no life in them. They can sit next to a man who is full of the Spirit of God, who is like a green bay tree, and who is bringing forth fruit; and yet they will not seek a similar blessing. Well, why this difference? Because God has poured water on him that was thirsty; that is the difference. One has been seeking this anointing, and he has received it; and when we want this above everything else God will surely give it to us.

The great question before us now is, *Do* we want it? I remember when I first went to England and gave a Bible reading – I think about the first that I gave in that country – a great many ministers were there, and I knew nothing about English theology, and was afraid I should run against their creeds: I was a little hampered, especially on this very subject about the gift of the Holy Spirit for service.

I particularly remember a Christian minister there who had his head bowed on his hand; I thought the good man was ashamed of everything I was saying, and of course that troubled me. At the close of my address he took his hat and away he went, and then I thought, 'Well, I shall never see him again.' At the next meeting I looked all around for him, and he was not there. At the next meeting I looked again, but he was absent: I thought my teaching must have given him offence. But a few days after that, at a large noon prayer meeting, a man stood up, and his face shone as if he had been up in the mountain with God: I looked at him, and to my great joy it was this brother. He said he was at that Bible reading, and he heard there was such a thing as having fresh power to preach the Gospel; he then made up his mind that if that was for him he would have it; he added that he went home and looked to the Master, and that he never had such a battle with himself in his life. He asked that God would show him the sinfulness of his heart, that he knew nothing about, and he just cried mightily to God that he might be emptied of himself and filled with the Spirit, and he said, 'God has answered my prayer.'

I met him in Edinburgh six months from that date, and he

told me he had preached the Gospel every night during that time; that he had not preached one sermon without some persons remaining behind for conversation; and that he had engagements four months ahead to preach the Gospel every night in different churches. I think you could have fired a cannon ball right through his church and not hit anyone before he received this anointing; but within thirty days afterwards the building was full and the aisles crowded. He had his bucket filled full of fresh water, and the people found it out, and came flocking to him from every quarter.

I tell you, You cannot get the stream higher than the fountain. What we need very specially is POWER. There was another man whom I have in my mind, and he said, 'I have heart disease; I cannot preach more than once a week': so he had a colleague to preach for him, and do the visiting. He was an old minister, and he could not do any visiting. He had heard of this anointing, and said, 'I should like to be anointed for my burial. I should like before I go hence to have the privilege of just once more preaching the Gospel with power.' He prayed that God would fill him with the Spirit. I met him not long after that, and he said, 'I have preached on an average eight times a week, and I have had conversions all along.' The Spirit came on him. I do not believe that man broke down at first with hard work, so much as from using the machinery without oil, without lubrication. It is not the hard work that breaks down ministers, but it is the toil of working without power. Oh that God may anoint His people! Not the ministry only, but every disciple.

Do not suppose pastors are the only labourers needing this. There is not a mother but needs it in her house to regulate her family; just as much as the minister needs it in the pulpit, or the Sunday-school teacher needs it in his Sunday-school. We all need it together; and let us not rest day nor night until we possess it. If that is the uppermost thought in our hearts, God will give it to us; He will grant us the blessing, if we just hunger and thirst for it, and say, 'God helping me, I will not rest until endued with power from on high.'

Master and Servant

There is a very sweet story of Elijah and Elisha; and I love to dwell upon it. The time had come for Elijah to be taken up, and he said to Elisha, 'You stay here at Gilgal, and I will go up to Bethel.' There was a theological seminary there, and some young students; and he wanted to see how they were getting along: but Elisha said, *'As the Lord liveth, and as thy soul liveth, I will not leave thee.'* And so Elisha just kept close to Elijah. They came to Bethel, and the sons of the prophets came out and said to Elisha, 'Do you know that your master is to be taken away?' And Elisha said, 'I know it; but you keep still.' Then Elijah said to Elisha, 'You remain at Bethel while I go to Jericho.' But Elisha said, *'As the Lord liveth, and as thy soul liveth, I will not leave thee.'* 'You shall not go without me,' says Elisha. And then I can imagine that Elisha just put his arm in that of Elijah, and they walked down together. I can, in imagination, see those two mighty men walking down to Jericho. When they arrived there, the sons of the prophets came and said to Elisha, 'Do you know that your master is to be taken away?' 'Hush! keep still,' says Elisha, 'I know it.' And then Elijah said to Elisha, 'Tarry here awhile; for the Lord hath sent me to Jordan.' But Elisha said, *'As the Lord liveth, and as thy soul liveth, I will not leave thee. You shall not go without me.'* And then Elisha came right close to Elijah; and as they went walking down, I imagine Elisha was after something.

When they came to the Jordan, Elijah took off his mantle and struck the waters, and they separated hither and thither, and the two passed through dry-shod; and fifty sons of the prophets came to look at them and watch them. They did not know but that Elijah would be taken up right in their sight. As they passed over Jordan, Elijah said to Elisha, 'Now, what do you want?' He knew he was after something. 'What can I do for you? Just make your request known.' And he said, 'I would like a double portion of thy spirit.' I can imagine, now that Elijah had given him a chance to ask, he said to himself, 'I will ask for enough.' Elisha had a good deal of the Spirit, but, says he, 'I want a double portion of thy spirit.' 'Well,' says Elijah, 'you have asked a hard thing,

but if you see me when I am taken up, you shall have it.' Do
you think you could have enticed Elisha from Elijah at that
moment? I can almost see the two arm in arm, walking
along; and as they walked, there came along the chariot of
fire, and before Elisha knew it, Elijah was caught up, and as
he went sweeping towards the throne, the servant cried, *'My
father! My father! the chariot of Israel and the horsemen
thereof!'* Elisha saw him no more. He picked up Elijah's
fallen mantle, and returning with that old garment of his
master's, he came to the Jordan and cried for Elijah's God;
and the waters separated hither and thither, and he passed
through dry-shod. Then the sons of the prophets lifted up
their voices and said, *'The Spirit of Elijah doth rest on
Elisha;'* and so it did – a double portion of it.

May the Spirit of Elijah, beloved reader, be upon us! If we
seek for it we shall have it. Oh, may the God of Elijah
answer by fire, and consume the spirit of worldliness in the
churches; burn up the dross; and make us whole-hearted
Christians! May that Spirit come upon us! Let that be our
prayer at our family altars and in our closets. Let us cry
mightily to God that we may have a double portion of the
Holy Spirit, and that we may not rest satisfied with this
worldly state of living. Let us, like Samson, shake ourselves,
and come out from the world, that we may have the power of
God.

෨   ෨

'A man may as well hew marble without tools, or paint without colours or instruments, or build without materials, as perform any acceptable service without the graces of the Spirit, which are both the materials and the instruments in the work.'   *Joseph Alleine*

'If we do not have the Spirit of God, it were better to shut the churches, to nail up the doors, to put a black cross on them, and say, "God have mercy on us!" If you ministers have not the Spirit of God, you had better not preach; and you people had better stay at home. I think I speak not too strongly when I say that a church in the land without the Spirit of God is rather a curse than a blessing. If you have not the Spirit of God, Christian worker, remember that you stand in somebody else's way; you are as a tree bearing no fruit, standing where another fruitful tree might grow. This is solemn work: the Holy Spirit – or nothing, and worse than nothing. Death and condemnation to a church that is not yearning after the Spirit, and crying and groaning until the Spirit has wrought mightily in her midst. He *is* here; He has never gone back since He descended at Pentecost. He is often grieved and vexed, for He is peculiarly jealous and sensitive, and the one sin never forgiven has to do with His blessed person: therefore let us be very tender towards Him; walk humbly before Him: wait on Him very earnestly; and resolve that about us there should be nothing knowingly continued which should prevent Him dwelling in us, and being with us henceforth and for ever.'   *C.H. Spurgeon*

෨   ෨

Chapter 3

Witnessing in Power

The subject of witness-bearing in the power of the Holy Ghost is not sufficiently understood by the Church. Until we have more intelligence on this point, we are labouring under great disadvantage. Now, if you will take your Bible and turn to John 15:26–27, you will find these words:

> 'When the Comforter is come, whom I will send unto you from the Father, even the Spirit of Truth, which proceedeth from the Father, He shall testify of Me; and ye also shall bear witness, because ye have been with Me from the beginning.'

Here we find what the Spirit is going to do, or what Christ said He would do when He came; namely, that the Spirit would testify of Him. And if you will turn to the second chapter of Acts you will find that when Peter stood up on the day of Pentecost, and testified of what Christ had done, the Holy Spirit came down and bore witness to that fact, and men were convicted and converted by hundreds and by thousands. So, then, man cannot preach effectively of himself. He must have the Spirit of God to give ability, and study God's Word, in order that he may testify according to the mind of the Spirit.

What is the Testimony?

If we keep back the Gospel of Christ, and do not bring Christ before the people, then the Spirit has not the opportunity to work. But the moment Peter stood up on the day of Pentecost and bore testimony to this one fact – that Christ died for sin; and that He had been raised again, and ascended into heaven – the Spirit came down to bear witness to the Person and Work of Christ.

He came down to bear witness to the fact that Christ was in heaven. And if it were not for the Holy Ghost bearing witness to the preaching of the facts of the Gospel, do you think that the Church would have lived during these last eighteen centuries? Do you believe that Christ's death, resurrection, and ascension, would not have been forgotten as soon as His birth, if it had not been for the fact that the Holy Spirit had come? Because it is very clear, that when John made his appearance on the borders of the wilderness, men had forgotten all about the birth of Jesus Christ. Just thirty short years. It was all gone.

They had forgotten the story of the shepherds who had watched their flocks by night on the hills of Bethlehem; they had forgotten the wonderful scene that took place when the Son of God was brought into the Temple, and the older prophets and prophetesses were there; they had forgotten about the wise men coming to Jerusalem to inquire where He was that was born King of the Jews. That story of His birth seemed to have just faded away; men had forgotten all about it: but when John made his appearance on the borders of the wilderness, it was brought back to their minds. And if it had not been for the Holy Ghost coming down to bear witness to Christ, to testify of His death and resurrection, these facts would have been forgotten as quickly as His birth had been.

Greater Work

The witness of the Spirit is the witness of power. Jesus said,

> *'He that believeth on Me, the works that I do shall he do also; and greater works than these shall he do, because I go unto My Father.'*

I used to stumble over that. I did not understand it. I

thought, What greater work could any man do than Christ had done? How could any one raise a dead man who had been laid away in the sepulchre for days, and who had already begun to turn back to dust; how could he call him forth with a word? But the longer I live the more I am convinced it is a greater thing to influence a man's will; the will of a man who is set against God; to have that will broken and brought into subjection to God's will: or, in other words, it is a greater thing to have power over a living, sinning, God-hating man, than to quicken the dead.

He who could create a world could speak a dead soul into life; but I think the greatest miracle this world has ever seen was the miracle at Pentecost. Here were men who surrounded the Apostles, full of prejudice, full of malice, full of bitterness; their hands, as it were dripping with the blood of the Son of God; and yet an unlettered man, a man whom they detested, a man whom they hated, stands up there and preaches the Gospel, and three thousand of them are immediately convicted and converted, become disciples of the Lord Jesus Christ, and are willing to lay down their lives for the Son of God. It may have been on that occasion that Stephen, the first martyr, was converted, and possibly also some of the other men who soon after gave up their lives for Christ. The work at Pentecost seems to me the greatest miracle this world has ever seen. But Peter did not labour alone; the Spirit of God was within him; hence the marvellous results.

The Jewish law required that there should be two witnesses; and we find that when Peter preached there was a second witness. Peter testified of Christ; and Christ had said, *'When the Comforter is come, even the Spirit of Truth ... He shall testify of Me.'* And the Holy Spirit and Peter both bore witness to the verities of our Lord's incarnation, ministry, death, and resurrection; and the result was that a multitude turned as with one heart unto the Lord. Our failure now is, that preachers ignore the Cross, and veil Christ with sapless sermons and superfine language. They do not present Him to the people plainly; and that, I believe, is why the Spirit of God does not work with power in our churches.

47

What we need is – to preach Christ, and present Him to a perishing world. The world can get on very well without you and me; but the world cannot get on without Christ; and therefore we must testify of Him. And the world, I believe, to-day is just hungering and thirsting for this divine, satisfying portion. Thousands and thousands are sitting in darkness, knowing not of this great Light: but when we begin to preach Christ honestly, faithfully, sincerely, and truthfully; holding Him up, and not ourselves; exalting Christ, and not our theories; presenting Christ, and not our opinions; advocating Christ, and not some false doctrine; then the Holy Ghost will come and bear witness. He will testify that what we say is true. When He comes He will confirm the Word with signs following. This is one of the strongest proofs that our Gospel is Divine; that it is of Divine origin; that not only did Christ teach these things, but that when leaving the world He had said concerning the Spirit, *'He shall glorify Me,'* and *'He shall testify of Me.'*

If you will just look at the second chapter of Acts – to that wonderful sermon that Peter preached – in the thirty-sixth verse you will read these words:

> *'Therefore let all the house of Israel know assuredly, that God hath made that same Jesus, whom ye have crucified, both Lord and Christ.'*

And when Peter said this, the Holy Ghost descended upon the people and testified of Christ – bore signal witness in demonstration that all this was true. And again, in the fortieth verse:

> *'And with many other words did He testify and exhort, saying, Save yourselves from this untoward generation.'*

With *'many other words'* did He testify; not only with these words that have been recorded, but with many other words.

The Sure Guide

Turn to the sixteenth chapter of John, in the thirteenth verse, and read:

> *'Howbeit, when He, the Spirit of Truth, is come, He will guide you into all truth; for He shall not speak of Himself; but whatsoever He shall hear, that shall He speak; and He will show you things to come.'*

He will *'guide you into all truth.'* Now there is no truth which we ought to know, which the Spirit of God will not guide us into if we will let Him; if we will yield ourselves up to be directed by the Spirit, and let Him lead us, He will guide us into all truth. It would have saved us from a great many dark hours if we had only been willing to let the Spirit of God be our counsellor and guide.

Lot would never have gone to Sodom if he had been guided by the Spirit of God. David never would have fallen into sin and had all that trouble with his family if he had been guided by the Spirit of God.

There are many Lots and Davids now-a-day. The churches are full of them. Men and women are in total darkness, because they have not been willing to be guided by the Spirit of God.

> *'He will guide you into all truth.'* *'He shall not speak of Himself.'*   (John 16:13)

He shall speak of the ascended glorified Christ.

What would be thought of a messenger, entrusted by an absent husband with a message for his wife or mother, who, on arrival, only talked of himself, and his conceits, and ignored both the husband and the message? You would simply deem it outrageous. What then must be the crime of the professed teacher who speaks of himself, or gives utterance to some insipid theory of his own, leaving out Christ and His Gospel! If we witness according to the Spirit, we must witness of Jesus.

The Holy Spirit is down here in this dark world to speak of

the Absent One; and He takes the things of Christ and brings them to our mind. He testifies of Christ; He guides us into the truth about Him.

Rappings in the Dark

I want to say right here, that I think in this day a great many children of God are turning aside and committing a grievous sin. I do not know that they think it a sin; but if we examine the Scriptures, I am sure we shall find that it is a great sin. We are told that the Comforter is sent into the world to 'guide us into all truth.' And if He is sent for that purpose, do we need any other guide? Need we hide in the darkness, consulting with mediums, who profess to call up the spirits of the dead? Do you know what the Word of God pronounces against that fearful sin? I believe it is one of the greatest sins we have to contend with at the present day. It is dishonouring to the Holy Spirit for me to go and summon up the dead and confer with them, even if it be possible.

I should like you to notice 1 Chronicles 10:13, 14:

> *'So Saul died for his transgression which he committed against the Lord, even against the Word of the Lord, which he kept not; and also for asking counsel of one that had a familiar spirit, to inquire of it; and inquired not of the Lord: therefore He slew him, and turned the kingdom unto David the Son of Jesse.'*

God slew him for this very sin. Of the two sins that are brought against Saul here, one is that he would not listen to the Word of God, and the second is that he consulted a familiar spirit. He was snared by this great evil, and sinned against God.

Saul grievously sinned in this. Yet there are a great many of God's professed children to-day, who think there is no harm in consulting a medium, who pretends to call up some of the departed to inquire of them.

But how dishonouring is this to God, who has sent the Holy Spirit into this world to guide us *'into all truth!'* There is not a thing that I need to know; there is not a thing that it is important for me to know; there is not a thing that I ought to know – but what the Spirit of God will reveal to me through the Word of God. And if I turn my back upon the Holy Spirit I am dishonouring the Spirit of God, and I am committing a grievous sin. You know that we read in the Gospel of Luke (16:19–31) of that rich man in the other world who wanted to have someone sent to his father's house to warn his five brothers. Christ said,

> *'They have Moses and the prophets; let them hear them;'*

and

> *'if they hear not Moses and the prophets, neither will they be persuaded though one rose from the dead.'*

'Moses and the prophets' – the part of the Bible then completed – that was enough. But a great many people now want something besides the Word of God, and are turning aside to these false lights.

Spirits that Peep and Mutter

There is a passage of Scripture which runs thus:

> *'When they shall say unto you, Seek unto them that have familiar spirits, and unto wizards that peep and that mutter; should not a people seek unto their God? for the living to the dead?'* (Isaiah 8:19)

What is that but table-rapping, and cabinet-hiding? If there were a message from God, do you think you would have to put out all the lights, or go into a dark room, in order to receive it? In secret my Master taught nothing (see John 18:20). God is not in that movement; and what we want, as children of God, is to keep ourselves from the evil.

51

And then notice the verse following, so often quoted out of its connection:

> *'To the law and to the testimony; if they speak not according to this word, it is because there is no light in them.'*
>
> (Isaiah 8:20)

Let us understand that if any man, or any woman, come to us with any doctrine that is not according to the law and the testimony, they are from the Evil One, and they are enemies of righteousness. They have 'no light' in them. Now you will find these people who are consulting familiar spirits – first and last – attack the Word of God. They do not believe it. Still a great many people say, You must hear both sides – but if a man should write me a most slanderous letter about my wife, I do not think I should feel called upon to read it; I should tear it up and throw it to the winds. Have I to read all the infidel books that are written, to hear both sides? Have I to take up a book that is a slander on my Lord and Master, who has redeemed me with His blood? Ten thousand times, No! I will not touch it.

> *'Now the Spirit speaketh expressly, that in the latter times some shall depart from the faith, giving heed to seducing spirits, and doctrines of devils.'*
>
> (1 Timothy 4:1)

That is pretty plain language is it not? – *'doctrines of devils.'* Again, *'speaking lies in hypocrisy; having their consciences seared with a hot iron.'* There are other passages of Scripture warning against every delusion of Satan. Let us ever remember the Spirit has been sent into the world to guide us into all truth. We want no other guide; He is enough. Some people say, 'Is not conscience a safer guide than the Word and the Spirit?' No, it is not. Some people seem not to have any conscience, and do not know what it means. Then education has a good deal to do with conscience. There are persons who will say that their conscience did not tell them that they had done wrong until after the wrong was done; but what we want, is something to tell us a thing is wrong before we do it.

Very often a man will go and commit some awful crime: and after he has committed it his conscience will wake up and lash and scourge him; it is too late then, the act is done.

The Unerring Guide

I am told by people who have been over the Alps, that if they are passing a dangerous place, the guide fastens them right to himself, and he just goes on before: they are fastened to the guide.

And so should the Christian be linked to his unerring Guide, and be safely upheld. Why, if a man were going through the Mammoth Cave in Kentucky it would be death to him if he strayed away from his guide – if separated from him he would certainly perish: there are pitfalls in that cave and a deep river; and there would be no chance for a man to find his way through the cave without a guide or a light. So there is no chance for us to get through the dark wilderness of this world alone. It is folly for a man or woman to think that they can get through this evil world without the light of God's Word and the guidance of the Divine Spirit. God sent Him to guide us through this great journey; and if we seek to work independent of Him, we shall be in peril of stumbling into the deep darkness of eternity's night.

But bear in mind the *Words* of the Spirit of God. If you want to be guided, you must study the Word; because the Word is the light of the Spirit. In John 14:26, we read:

> *'But the Comforter, which is the Holy Ghost, whom the Father will send in My name, He shall teach you all things, and bring all things to your remembrance, whatsoever I have said unto you.'*

Again, in John 16:13:

> *'Howbeit when He, the Spirit of truth, is come, He will guide you into all truth: for He shall not speak of Himself; but whatsoever He shall hear, that shall He speak: and He will show you things to come.'*

'He Will Show You Things to Come'

A great many people seem to think that the Bible is out of date, that it is an old book, and that it has passed its day. They say it was very good for the dark ages, and that there is some very good history in it; but that it was not intended for the present time; that we are living in a very enlightened age, and that men can get on very well without the Old Book; that we have outgrown it. They think we have no use for it, because it is an old book. Now you might just as well say that the sun, which has shone so long, is now so old that it is out of date; and that whenever a man builds a house he need not put any windows in it, because we now have a newer and better light: we have gaslight and this new electric light; these are something new. I would advise people, if they think the Bible is old and worn out, when they build houses not to put any windows in them, but just to light them with this new electric light: that is something new; and this is what many are anxious for.

People talk about this Book as if they understood it; but we do not know all about it yet. The press gives us the daily news of what has taken place. This Bible, however, tells us *what is about to take place*. This *is* new; we have the news here in this Book. This tells us of the things that will surely come to pass; and that is a great deal newer than anything in the newspapers. It tells us that the Spirit shall teach us *'all things'*; not only guide us into all truth, but teach us all things. He teaches us how to pray; and I do not think there has ever upon this sin-cursed earth been a prayer that has been indited by the Holy Spirit, but what was answered. There is much praying that is not indited by the Holy Spirit. In former years I was very ambitious to get rich. I used to pray for one hundred thousand dollars: that was my aim; and I used to say, 'God does not answer my prayer; He does not make me rich.' But I had no warrant for such a prayer. Yet a good many people pray in that way: they think that they pray; but they do not pray according to the Scriptures. The Spirit of God has nothing to do with their prayers, and such prayers are not the outcome of His teaching.

It is the Spirit who teaches us how to answer our enemies.

If a man strikes me, I should not pull out a revolver and shoot him. The Spirit of the Lord does not teach me to revenge myself; He does not teach me that it is necessary to draw the sword, and cut a man down in order to defend my rights. Some people say, You are a coward if you do not strike back. Christ says, Turn the other cheek to him who smites. I would rather take Christ's teaching than any other. I do not think a man gains much by arming himself with weapons for defence. There has been life enough sacrificed in America to teach men a lesson in this matter. The Word of God is a much better protection than the revolver. We had better take the Word of God to protect us, by accepting its teaching, and living out its precepts.

An Aid to Memory

It is a great comfort to us to remember that another office of the Spirit is to bring the teaching of Jesus to our remembrance. Our Lord's promise was:

> *'He shall teach you all things, and bring all things to your remembrance.'* (John 14:26)

How striking that is! I think there are many Christians who have realized this in their experience. They have been testifying, and found that while talking for Christ the Spirit has just brought into mind some of the sayings of the Lord Jesus Christ, and their mind was soon filled with the Word of God. When we have the Spirit resting upon us, we can speak with authority and power, and the Lord will bless our testimony and honour our work. I believe the reason why God makes use of so few in the Church, is because there is not in them the power that God can use. He is not going to use our ideas: but we must have the Word of God hid in our hearts; and then, the Holy Spirit inflaming us, we shall be enabled to give testimony which will be rich, and fresh, and sweet, and the Lord's Word will vindicate itself in blessed results.

God wants to use us; God wants to make us channels of blessing. But some of us are in such a condition that He cannot use us. That is the trouble. There are so many men who have no testimony for the Lord: if they speak, they speak without saying anything; and if they pray, their prayer is powerless: they do not plead in prayer; their prayer is just a few set phrases that you have heard too often. Now, what we want is to be so full of the Word, that the Spirit coming upon us shall bring to our mind – bring to our remembrance – the words of the Lord Jesus.

In 1 Corinthians 2:9, it is written:

> *'Eye hath not seen, nor ear heard, neither have entered into the heart of man, the things which God hath prepared for them that love Him.'*

We hear that passage so often quoted in prayer – many a man weaves it into his prayer and stops right there. And the moment you talk about Heaven they say, 'Oh, we know nothing about Heaven, the knowledge of it hath not entered into the heart of man; eye hath not seen; it is all speculation; we have nothing to do with it'; and they say they just quote what is written:

> *'Eye hath not seen, nor ear heard, neither have entered into the heart of man, the things which God hath prepared for them that love Him.'*

What next? *'But God hath revealed them unto us by His Spirit.'* You see, the Lord hath revealed them unto us: *'For the Spirit searcheth all things; yea, the deep things of God.'* That is just what the Spirit does.

Long-sighted or Short-sighted

The Spirit brings to our mind what God has in store for us. Some time ago, I heard a man speaking about Abraham. He said, 'Abraham was not tempted by the well-watered plains of Sodom, for Abraham was what you might call a long-sighted man: he had his eyes set on the *"city which hath foundations, whose Builder and Maker is God"*.' But Lot was a short-sighted man: and there are many people in the Church who are very short-sighted; they only see those things right around them which they think good. Abraham was long-sighted; he had glimpses of the eternal City. Moses was long-sighted: he left the palaces of Egypt, and identified himself with God's people – poor people, who were slaves; but he had something in view yonder; he could see something God had in store. Again, there are some people who are a sort of mixture of long-sightedness and short-sightedness. I have a friend who has one eye that is long-sighted, while the other is short-sighted; and I think the Church is full of this kind of people. They want one eye for the world, and the other for the Kingdom of God. Therefore, everything is blurred; one eye is long-sighted, and the other is short-sighted: all is confusion; and they *'see men as trees walking.'* The Church is filled with that sort of people.

Stephen was long-sighted; he looked clear into heaven; even when he was dying, his enemies could not convince him that Christ had not ascended to heaven. *'Look! look yonder!'* he says; *'I see Him over there; He is on the throne, standing at the right hand of God;'* and he looked clear into heaven. The world had no temptation for him; he had put the world under his feet. Paul was another of those long-sighted men; he had been caught up and heard unspeakable words impossible for him to utter; words wonderful and glorious.

I tell you, when the Spirit of God is on us, the world looks very empty; the world has a very small hold upon us, and we begin to let go our hold of it. When the Spirit of God is upon us, we shall just let go the things of time, and lay hold of things eternal. This is the Church's need to-day. We want the Spirit to come in mighty power, and consume all the vile dross there is in us. Oh that the Spirit of fire may come down and burn everything in us that is contrary to God's blessed Word and will!

In John 14:16, we read of the Comforter. This is the first time He is spoken of as the Comforter. Christ had been the Comforter. God had sent Him to comfort the sorrowing. It had been prophesied of Jesus, seven hundred years before:

'The Spirit of the Lord God is upon Me, because the Lord hath anointed Me to preach the Gospel to the poor; He hath sent Me to heal the broken-hearted.'

(Luke 4:18; Isaiah 61:1)

You cannot heal the broken-hearted without the Comforter. But the world would not have the first Comforter, and so they rose up and took Him to Calvary and put Him to death. But on going away He said,

'I will send you another Comforter; you shall not be comfortless; be of good cheer, little flock; it is the Father's good pleasure to give you the kingdom.'

All these precious passages are brought to the remembrance of God's people, and they help them to rise out of the fog and mist of this world. Oh, what a comforter is the Holy Spirit of God!

The Faithful Friend

The Holy Spirit tells a man of his faults, in order to lead him to a better life. In John 16:8, we read: *'He will reprove* [or, convince] *the world of sin.'* Now, there are a class of people who do not like this part of the Spirit's work. Do you know why? Because He convicts *them* of sin; and they do not like that. What they want is someone to speak comforting words and make everything pleasant; to keep everything quiet; to tell them there is peace when there is war; to tell them it is light when it is dark; to tell them that everything is growing better – that the world is getting on amazingly in goodness – that it is becoming better all the time: that is the kind of preaching they seek for. Men think they are a great deal better than their fathers were. That suits human nature, for human nature is full of pride. Men will strut around and say, 'Yes, I believe that; the world is improving. I am a good deal better man than my father was; my father was too strict; he was one of those old Puritanical men who were so rigid. Oh, we are getting on; we are more liberal. My father would not

58

think of going out riding on Sunday, but we do it; we will trample the laws of God under our feet; we are better than our fathers.'

That is the kind of talking which some dearly love; and there are preachers who tickle such itching ears. When you bring the Word of God to bear upon men, and the Spirit drives it home, then they say, 'I do not like that kind of preaching; I will never go to hear that man again'; and sometimes they will get up and stamp their way out of church before the speaker has finished; they do not like it. But when the Spirit of God is at work, He convicts men of sin. *'When He is come, He will reprove the world of sin, and of right-eousness, and of judgment; of sin'* – not because men swear, or lie, or steal, or get drunk, or murder – but, says Christ, *'of sin, because they believe not on Me.'*

The Climax Sin

That is the sin of the world. Why, a great many people think that unbelief is a sort of misfortune; but they do not realize, if you will allow me the expression, that it is the damning sin of the world to-day. That is what unbelief is, the mother of all sin. There would not be a drunkard walking the streets, if it were not for unbelief; there would not be a harlot walking the streets, if it were not for unbelief; there would not be a murderer, if it were not for unbelief: it is the germ of all sin. Do not for a moment think that unbelief is simply a misfortune; but just bear in mind it is an awful sin: and may the Holy Spirit convince every reader that unbelief is making God a liar! Many a man has knocked down another in the street because he has told him he was a liar. Unbelief is giving God the lie; that is the plain English of it. Some people seem to boast of their unbelief: they seem to think it is quite respectable to be an infidel and doubt God's Word; and they will vainly boast and say, 'I have intellectual difficulties: I cannot believe.'

Oh that the Spirit of God may come and convict men of sin! That is what we need – His convicting power. I am so thankful that God has not put that work of convicting into our hands. We have not to convict men. If we had, I should get discouraged, and give up preaching, and go back to business. It is my work to preach and hold up the Cross and testify of Christ; but it is the Spirit's work to convict men of sin, and lead them to Christ. One thing I have noticed – that some conversions do not amount to anything; that if a man professes to be converted without conviction of sin, he proves to be one of those stony-ground hearers who do not bring forth much fruit. The first little wave of persecution, the first breath of opposition, and the man is back in the world again.

Let us pray, dear Christian friends, that God may carry on a deep and thorough work, that men may be so convicted of sin that they cannot rest in unbelief. Let us pray God that it may be a thorough work in the land. I would a great deal rather see a hundred men thoroughly converted, truly born of God, than to see a thousand professed conversions where the Spirit of God has not convicted of sin. Do not let us cry, *'Peace! peace! when there is no peace.'* Do not go to the man who is living in sin, and tell him all he has to do is to stand right up and make a profession, without any hatred for sin. Let us ask God first to show every man the plague of his own heart, that the Spirit may convict him of sin. Then will the work in our hands be real and deep, and abide the fiery trial which will try every man's labour.

Thus far, we have found the work of the Spirit is to impart life, to implant hope, to give liberty, to testify of Christ, to guide into all truth, to teach us all things, to comfort believers, and to convict the world of sin.

'Holy Spirit, faithful Guide,
Ever near the Christian's side;
Gently lead us by the hand,
Pilgrims in a desert land:
Weary souls for aye rejoice,
While they hear that sweetest voice,
Whisp'ring softly, "Wanderer, come!
Follow Me, I'll guide thee home."

'Ever present, truest Friend,
Ever near Thine aid to lend,
Leave us not to doubt and fear,
Groping on in darkness drear:
When the storms are raging sore,
Hearts grow faint, and hopes give o'er;
Whisper softly, "Wanderer, come!
Follow Me, I'll guide thee home."

'When our days of toil shall cease,
Waiting still for sweet release,
Nothing left but heaven and prayer,
Trusting that our names are there,
Wading deep the dismal flood,
Pleading nought but Jesus' blood;
Whisper softly, "Wanderer, come!
Follow Me, I'll guide thee home."'

∽   ∾

'*"Ye are not your own." "Your bodies are the temples of the Holy Ghost."* Is that an unmeaning metaphor, or an over-worded expression? When the Holy Spirit enters the soul, heaven enters with Him. The heart is compared to a temple. God never enters without His attendants: **repentance** cleanses the house; **faith** provides for the house; **watchfulness**, like the porter, takes care of it; **prayer** is a lively messenger, learns what is wanted, and then goes for it; **faith** tells him where to go, and he never goes in vain; **joy** is the musician of this temple, tuning to the praises of God and the Lamb. And this terrestrial temple shall be removed to the celestial world, for the trumpet shall sound, and the dead shall be raised.'

Rowland Hill

∽   ∾

Chapter 4

Power in Operation

The power we have been considering is the Presence of the Holy Spirit. He is omnipotent. Power in operation is the action of the Spirit or the fruit of the Spirit. This we shall now consider. Paul writes in Galatians 5:16–18, 22–26:

'This I say then, Walk in the Spirit, and ye shall not fulfil the lust of the flesh. For the flesh lusteth against the Spirit, and the Spirit against the flesh: and these are contrary, the one to the other; so that ye cannot do the things that ye would. But if ye be led of the Spirit, ye are not under the law.'

'The fruit of the Spirit is love, joy, peace, long-suffering, gentleness, goodness, faith, meekness, temperance; against such there is no law. And they that are Christ's have crucified the flesh with the affections and lusts. If we live in the Spirit, let us also walk in the Spirit. Let us not be desirous of vain-glory, provoking one another, envying one another.'

Now, *there* is a life of perfect peace, perfect joy, and perfect love: and that ought to be the aim of every child of God; that ought to be the standard; and no Christian should rest until he has attained that position. That is God's standard, which He wants all His children to reach. These nine graces mentioned in this chapter in Galatians can be divided in this way: Love and peace, and joy, are all God-ward, toward God. God looks for that fruit from each one of His children; and that is the kind of fruit which is acceptable with Him. Without that we cannot please God. He wants, above everything else, that we possess love, peace, and joy. And then the next three – goodness, long-suffering, and gentleness – are toward man. That should be our outward life toward those with whom we are coming in contact continually – daily, hourly. The next three – faith, temperance, meekness – are in relation to ourselves. And in that way we can just take the three divisions, and it will be of some help to us.

The first thing that meets us as we enter the kingdom of God, you might say, are these first three graces,

Love, Peace and Joy

When a man who has been living in sin turns from his sins, and turns to God with all his heart, he is met on the threshold of the divine life by these sister graces. The love of God is shed abroad in his heart by the Holy Ghost. The peace of God comes at the same time, and also the joy of the Lord. We can all put the test to ourselves as to whether we have these graces. They are not anything that we can make. The great trouble with many is that they are trying to make these graces. They are trying to create love; they are trying to create peace; they are trying to create joy. But these are not products of human planting. To produce them of ourselves is impossible. Their production is an act of God. They come from above. It is God who speaks the word, and gives the love; it is God who gives the peace; it is God who gives the joy. And we possess all by receiving Jesus Christ by faith into the heart; for when Christ comes by faith into the heart, then the Spirit is there; and if we have the Spirit, we shall have the fruit of the Spirit.

If the whole Church of God could live as the Lord would have her live, Christianity would be the mightiest power this world has ever seen. It is the low standard of Christian life that is causing so much trouble. There are a great many stunted Christians in the Church; their lives are stunted; they are like trees planted in poor ground – the earth is hard and stony, and the roots cannot find the rich loamy soil needed. Such believers have not grown in these sweet graces.

Peter, in his second epistle (1:5), writes:

> *'And besides this, giving all diligence, add to your faith, virtue; and to virtue, knowledge; and to knowledge, temperance; and to temperance, patience; and to patience, godliness; and to godliness, brotherly kindness; and to brotherly kindness, charity. For if these things be in you and abound, they make you that ye shall neither be barren nor unfruitful in the knowledge of our Lord Jesus Christ.'*

Now, if we have these things in us, I believe that we shall be constantly bringing forth fruit that will be acceptable with God. It will not be just a little fruit every now and then, when we spur ourselves up and work ourselves up into a certain state of mind or into an excited condition, and labour a little while, and then become cold, and discouraged, and disheartened. We shall be neither unfruitful nor barren; we shall be bringing forth fruit constantly; we shall grow in grace, and be filled with the Spirit of God.

What Wins

A great many parents have inquired of me how to win their children. They say they have talked with them; and sometimes have scolded them and have lectured them; and yet have signally failed. I think there is no way so sure to win to Christ our families and our neighbours, and those about whom we are anxious, as just to adorn the doctrine of Jesus Christ in our lives, and grow in all these graces of the Spirit. If we have peace, and joy, and love, and gentleness, and goodness and temperance; not only being temperate in what we drink, but also in what we eat, and temperate in our language, guarded in our expressions; if we just live in our homes, as the Lord would have us, an even Christian life day by day, we shall have a quiet and silent power proceeding from us, that will constrain those around to believe on the Lord Jesus Christ.

But an uneven life, hot to-day and cold to-morrow, will only repel. Many are watching God's people. It is just the very worst thing that can happen to those whom we want to win to Christ, to see us, at any time, in a cold, backslidden state. This is not the normal condition of the Church; it is not God's intention: He would have us growing in all Christian graces. And the only true, happy, Christian life is to be growing, constantly growing, in the love and favour of God, growing in all these delightful graces of the Spirit.

Even the vilest, the most impure, acknowledge the power of goodness; they recognize the fruit of the Spirit. It may condemn their lives, and cause them to say bitter things at times; but down deep in their hearts they know that the man or woman who is living that kind of life, is superior to them. The world does not satisfy them; and if we can show the world that Jesus Christ does satisfy us in our present life, this will be more powerful than the eloquent words of professional reformers. A man may preach with the eloquence of an angel; but if he does not live what he preaches, and act out in his home and his business what he professes, his testimony goes for nought, and the people say it is all hypocrisy after all – it is all a sham.

Words are very empty, if there is nothing at the back of them. Your testimony is poor and worthless, if there is not at the back of that testimony a record consistent with what you profess. What we need is to pray to God to lift us up out of this low, cold, formal state that we have been living in; that we may live in the atmosphere of God continually, and that the Lord may lift upon us the light of His countenance; and that so we may shine in this world, reflecting His grace and glory.

The first of the graces spoken of in Galatians, and the last mentioned in Peter, is Charity or Love. We cannot serve God – we cannot work for God – unless we have love. That is the key which unlocks the human heart. If I can prove to a man that I come to him out of pure love – it will not be long before that man is stirred: if a mother shows by her actions that it is pure love that prompts her in advising her boy to lead a different life – not a selfish love, but her desire for the glory of God – it will not be long before that mother's influence will be felt by that boy, and he will begin to think about the matter; because true love touches the heart quicker than anything else.

The Power of Love

Love is the badge that Christ gave His disciples. Some put on one sort of badge and some another. Some put on a strange kind of dress, that they may be known as Christians; and some wear a crucifix, or something of the sort, that they may be recognized as making a Christian profession. But love is the only badge by which the disciples of our Lord Jesus Christ are to be known. *'By this shall all men know that ye are My disciples, if ye have love one to another.'*

Therefore, though a man stand before an audience and speak with the eloquence of a Demosthenes, or of the greatest living orator, if there be no love at the back of his words, they are but sounding brass and a tinkling cymbal. I would recommend all Christians to read the thirteenth chapter of the first Epistle to the Corinthians constantly, abiding in it day and night, not spending a night or a day there, but just going in there and spending all their time – summer and winter, twelve months in the year; then the power of Christ and Christianity would be felt as it never has been in the history of the world. See what this chapter says:

> *'Though I speak with the tongues of men and of angels, and have not charity, I am become as sounding brass, or a tinkling cymbal. And though I have the gift of prophecy, and understand all mysteries, and all knowledge; and though I have all faith, so that I could remove mountains; and have not charity, I am nothing.'*

A great many are praying for Faith: they want extraordinary faith; they want remarkable faith. They forget that Love exceeds Faith. The **Charity** spoken of in the above verses, is **Love**, the fruit of the Spirit, the great motive-power of life. What the Church of God needs to-day is Love – more love to God, and more love to our fellow-men. If we love God more, we shall love our fellow-men more. There is no doubt about that.

I used to think that I should like to have lived in the days of the prophets; that I should like to have been one of the prophets, to prophesy, and to see the glories of heaven and describe them to men; but, as I understand the Scriptures now, I would a good deal rather live in the thirteenth chapter of 1st Corinthians, and have this love that Paul speaks of burning in my soul like an unquenchable flame, so that I might reach men and win them for heaven.

A man may have wonderful knowledge, and be capable of unravelling the mysteries of the Bible, and yet be as cold as an icicle. He may glisten like the snow in the sun. Sometimes you may have wondered why it was that certain ministers who had such wonderful magnetism, who had such a marvellous command of language, and who preached with such mental power, have not had more conversions.

I believe, if the truth were known, you would find no divine love at the back of their words, no pure love in their sermons. You may preach like an angel – Paul says, *'with the tongues of men and of angels'* – but if you have not love, it amounts to nothing. *'And though I bestow all my goods to feed the poor'* – a man may be very charitable, and give away all his goods; a man may give all he has; but if it is not the love of God which prompts the gift, it will not be acceptable with God. *'And though I give my body to be burned, and have not charity'* – have not love – *'it profiteth me nothing.'* A man may go to the stake for his principles; he may go to the stake for what he believes; but if it is not love to God which actuates him, it will not be acceptable to God.

Love's Wonderful Effects

'Charity suffereth long, and is kind; charity envieth not; charity vaunteth not itself; is not puffed up:

'Doth not behave itself unseemly; seeketh not her own; is not easily provoked; thinketh no evil.'

That is the work of Love. It is not easily provoked. Now if a man has no love of God in his heart, how easy it is to become offended! Perhaps with the Church: because some members of the church do not treat him quite right, or some men of the church do not bow to him on the street, he takes offence; and that is the last you see of him. Love is long-suffering. If I love the Lord Jesus Christ, these little things are not going to separate me from His people. They are like the dust in the balance. Nor will the cold, formal treatment of hypocrites in the church quench that love I have in my heart for Him. If this love is in the heart, and the fire is burning on the altar, we shall not be all the time finding fault with other people, or criticizing what they have done.

Fault-finding

Love will rebuke evil, but will not rejoice in it. Love will be impatient of sin, but patient with the sinner. To contract the habit of constantly finding fault, is very damaging to spiritual life; it is about the lowest and meanest position a man can take. I never saw a man who was aiming to do the best work, but that there might be some improvement. I never did anything in my life – I never addressed an audience – but what I afterwards felt I could have done better; and I have often upbraided myself that I had not done better. But to sit down and find fault with other people when we are doing nothing ourselves, not lifting our hands to save a single person, is all wrong, and is the opposite of holy, patient, divine love.

Love is forbearance; and what we want is to get this spirit of criticism and fault-finding out of the Church and out of our hearts. Let each one of us live as if we had to answer for ourselves, and not for the community, at the last day. If we are living according to the thirteenth chapter of this Epistle, we shall not be all the time finding fault with other people. *'Love suffereth long, and is kind.'* Love forgets itself, and does not harp upon itself.

The woman who came to Christ with that alabaster box, I venture to say, never thought of herself. Little did she know what an act she was performing. It was just her love for her Master. She forgot the surroundings; she forgot everyone else who was there; she broke that box and poured the ointment upon Him, and filled the house with its odour. The act, as a memorial, has come down these eighteen hundred years. It is right here – the perfume of that box is in the world to-day. That ointment was worth forty or fifty dollars; no small sum in those days for a poor woman. Judas sold the Son of God for about fifteen or twenty dollars. But what this woman gave to Christ was everything that she had; and she became so occupied with Jesus Christ that she did not consider what people would say.

So when we act with a single eye for the glory of our Lord, not finding fault with everything about us, but doing what we can in the power of this love, then will our deeds for God speak; and the world will acknowledge that we have been with Jesus, and that this glorious love has been shed abroad in our hearts.

What we want then, is to have love for Christ; to have love for His Word; and to have love for the Church of God: and when we have love, and are living in a loving spirit, we shall not be in the spirit of finding fault and working mischief.

After Love, What?

After Love comes Peace. A great many people are trying to make peace. But that has already been done. God has not left it for us to do; all that we have to do is to enter into it. It is a condition. And instead of our trying to make peace and to work for peace, we must cease from all that, and sweetly enter into peace.

If I discover a man in the cellar complaining because there is no light there, and because it is cold and damp, I say: 'My friend, come up out of the cellar. There is a good warm sun up here: we have a beautiful spring day, and it is warm, cheerful, and light; come up and enjoy it.' He might perhaps reply: 'Oh no, sir; I am trying to see if I can make light down here; I am trying to work myself into a warm feeling.' And there he is working away; and he may have been at it for a

70

whole week. I can imagine that my reader will smile; but you may be smiling at your own picture; for this is the condition of many whom I daily meet, who are trying to do this very thing – they are trying to work themselves into peace and joyful feelings.

Peace is a condition into which we enter; it is a state: and instead of our trying to make peace, let us believe what God's Word declares, that peace has already been made by the blood of the Cross. Christ has made peace for us; and now what He desires is that we believe it and enter into it. Now, the only thing that can keep us from peace is sin. God turneth the way of the wicked upside down (Psalm 146:9). *'There is no peace, saith my God, to the wicked'* (Isaiah 48:22; 57:21). They are like the troubled sea that cannot rest, casting up filth and mire all the while. But peace with God by faith in Jesus Christ – peace through the knowledge of forgiven sin – is like a rock; the waters go dashing and surging past it, but it abides.

When we find peace, we shall not find it on the ground of innate goodness; it comes from without ourselves, but into us. In John 16:33, we read:

> *'These things I have spoken unto you, that in Me ye might have peace.'*

That in Me ye might have peace. Jesus Christ is the author of peace. He procured peace. His gospel is the gospel of peace.

> *'Behold, I bring you good tidings of great joy which shall be to all people; for unto you is born this day, in the city of David, a Saviour;'*

and then came that chorus from heaven,

> *'Glory to God in the highest! and on earth peace!'*
> (Luke 2:10, 11, 14)

He brought peace.

'In the world ye shall have tribulation: but be of good cheer; I have overcome the world.' (John 16:33)

How true that in the world we have tribulation. Are you in tribulation? Are you in trouble? Are you in sorrow? Remember this is our lot. Paul had tribulation, and others have shared in grief. Nor shall we be exempt from trial. But within, peace may reign undisturbed. If sorrow is our lot, peace is our legacy. Jesus gives peace. And do you know there is a good deal of difference between His peace and our peace? Anyone can disturb our peace; but they cannot disturb His peace. That is the kind of peace He has left us. Nothing can offend those who trust in Christ.

Not Easily Offended

In Psalm 119:165, we read:

'Great peace have they which love Thy law; and nothing shall offend them.'

The study of God's Word will secure peace. Take those Christians who are rooted and grounded in the Word of God, and you will find they have great peace. It is those who do not study their Bible, and do not know their Bible, who are easily offended when some little trouble comes, or some little persecution: then their peace is all disturbed; just a little breath of opposition, and their peace is all gone.

Sometimes I am amazed to see how little it takes to drive all peace and comfort from some people. Some slandering tongue will readily succeed in doing it. But if we have the peace of God, the world cannot take that peace from us. It cannot give it; it cannot destroy it. We have to obtain it from a source above the world; it is the peace which Christ gives. *'Great peace have they which love Thy law; and nothing shall offend them.'* Christ says, *'Blessed is he, whosoever shall not be offended in Me'* (Matthew 11:6). Now, if you will notice, wherever there is a Bible-taught Christian, one who has the Bible well-marked, and daily feeds upon the Word by

72

prayerful meditation, he will not be easily offended. Such people are growing and working all the while.

But it is those people who never open their Bibles – those people who never study the Scriptures – who become offended, and are wondering why they are having such a hard time. They are the persons who tell you that Christianity is not what it has been recommended to them as being; that they have found it was not all that we claim it to be. The real trouble is – they have not done as the Lord has told them to do. They have neglected the Word of God. If they had been studying the Word of God, they would not be in that condition. If they had been studying the Word of God, they would not have wandered for these years away from God, living on the husks of the world. But the trouble is, they have neglected to care for the new life: they have not fed it; and the poor soul, being starved, sinks into weakness and decay, and is easily stumbled or offended.

I met a man who confessed his soul had fed on nothing for forty years. 'Well,' said I, 'that is pretty hard for the soul – giving it nothing to feed on!' And that man is but a type of thousands and tens of thousands to-day; their poor souls are starving. This body that we inhabit for a day, and then leave, we take good care of; we feed it three times a day, and we clothe it, and take care of it, and deck it: by-and-by it is going into the grave to be eaten up by the worms; but the inner man, that is to live on and on and on for ever, we suffer to become lean and starved.

Sweet Words

In Numbers 6:22–26, we read:

> *'And the Lord spake unto Moses, saying: Speak unto Aaron and unto his sons, saying, On this wise ye shall bless the children of Israel, saying unto them: The Lord bless thee and keep thee; the Lord make His face shine upon thee, and be gracious unto thee; the Lord lift up His countenance upon thee, and give thee peace!'*

I think these are about as sweet verses as any we find in the Old Testament. I marked them years ago in my Bible; and many times I have turned over and read them. *'The Lord lift up His countenance upon thee, and give thee peace!'* The Jewish salutation used to be, as a man went into a house, 'Peace be upon this house;' and as he left the house the host would say, 'Go in peace.'

Then again, in John 14:27, we read that Jesus said:

> *'Peace I leave with you; My peace I give unto you; not as the world giveth give I unto you. Let not your heart be troubled, neither let it be afraid.'*

This is the precious legacy of Jesus to all His followers. Every man, every woman, every child, who believes in Him, may share in this portion. Christ has willed it to them, and His peace is theirs.

This, then, is our Lord's purpose and promise. *'My peace I give unto you.'* I give it, and I am not going to take it away again; I am going to leave it with you.

> *'Not as the world giveth give I unto you. Let not your heart be troubled, neither let it be afraid.'*

But you know, when some men make their wills and bequeath their property, there are some sharp, shrewd lawyers who will get hold of the will and break it all to pieces; they will go into court and break the will, and the jury will set the will aside, and the money goes into another channel. Now this will that Christ has made, neither devil nor man can break. He has promised to give us peace. And there are thousands of witnesses who can say: 'I have my part of that legacy: I have peace; I came to Him for peace, and I received it; I came to Him in darkness – I came to Him in trouble and sorrow – I was passing under a deep cloud of affliction, and I came to Him – and He said, *"Peace, be still!"* And from that hour peace has reigned in my soul.' Yes, thousands who have accepted Christ's invitation, *'Come unto Me, all ye that labour and and are heavy-laden,'* have realised the truth of the precious promise, *'I will give you rest'* (Matthew 11:28). They found **Rest** when they came. He is the Author of rest; He is the Author of peace. No power can break that will and testament. Unbelief may question it; but Jesus Christ rose to execute His own will, and it is in vain for man to contest it. Infidels and sceptics may tell us that Christ's gospel is all a myth, and that there is nothing in it, and yet the glorious tidings are ever repeated, *'Peace on earth, good-will to men!'* and the poor and needy, the sad and sorrowful, are made partakers of it.

So, my reader, you need not wait for peace any longer. All you have to do is to enter into it to-day. You need not try to make peace. It is a false idea; you cannot make it. Peace is already made by Jesus Christ, and is now declared unto you.

Peace Declared

When France and England were at war, a French vessel had gone off on a long voyage, a whaling voyage: on their way back, the crew were short of water, and being now near an English port, they wanted to procure a supply; but they were afraid that they would be taken captive if they went into that port: some people in the port saw them, noticed their signal of distress, and sent word to them that they need not be afraid, that the war was over, and peace had been declared. But they could not make those sailors believe it; and the poor fellows dared not go into port, although they were out of water. At last they made up their minds that they had better go in and surrender up their cargo, and lose their freedom, than perish out at sea for want of water; but when they went into the harbour they found out that peace had been really declared, and that what had been told them was true.

In like manner, there are a great many people who do not believe the glad tidings that peace has been made. Jesus Christ made peace on the Cross. He satisfied the claims of the law; and this law which condemns you and me has been fulfilled by Jesus Christ. He has made peace; and now He wants us just to enjoy it, just to believe it. Nor is there anything to hinder us from doing this, if we will. We can enter into that blessing now, and have perfect peace. The promise is:

> *'Thou wilt keep him in perfect peace whose mind is stayed on Thee; because he trusteth in Thee. Trust ye in the Lord for ever; for in the Lord Jehovah is everlasting strength.'* (Isaiah 26: 3, 4)

Now, as long as our minds are stayed on our own dear selves, we shall never have peace. Some people think more of themselves than of all the rest of the world. It is self in the morning, self at noon, and self at night. It is self when they wake up, and self when they go to bed; and they are all the time looking at themselves, and thinking about themselves, instead of *'looking unto Jesus.'* Faith is an outward look. Faith does not look within; it looks without. It is not what I think, nor what I feel, nor what I have done; but it is what Jesus Christ is, and what He has done. And so we should trust in Him who is our strength, and whose strength will never fail. After Christ rose from the grave, John tells us that three times He met His disciples and said unto them, *'Peace be unto you'* (John 20:19, 21, 26). There is peace for the conscience through His blood, and peace for the heart in His love.

The Secret of Joy

Remember then, that Love is power; and Peace is power. But now I will call attention to another fruit of the Spirit; and this too is power – the grace of **Joy**. It is the privilege, I believe, of every Christian to walk in the light, as God is in the light, and to have that peace which will be flowing unceasingly as we keep busy about His work. And it is our privilege to be full of the joy of the Lord. We read that when Philip went down to Samaria and preached, there was great joy in the city. Why? Because the inhabitants believed the glad tidings. And that is the natural order – joy in believing. When we believe the glad tidings, joy comes into our souls.

We are also told that our Lord sent out the seventy, and that they went forth preaching salvation in the name of Jesus Christ, and the result was that a great many were blessed; and the seventy returned, we are told, with great joy; and when they came back they said that the very devils were subject to them, through His name. The Lord seems just to check them in this one thing, when He says,

> '*Rejoice not that the spirits are subject unto you; but rather rejoice, because your names are written in heaven.*'
> (Luke 10:20)

There is assurance for you. They had something to rejoice in now. God does not ask us to rejoice over nothing; but He gives us good ground for our joy.

What would you think of a man or woman who seemed very happy to-day, and full of joy, and could not tell you what made them so? Suppose I should meet a man in the street, and he was so full of joy that he should seize hold of both my hands and say, 'Bless the Lord, I am so full of joy!' 'What makes you so full of joy?' 'Well, I don't know.' 'You don't know?' 'No, I don't; but I am so joyful that I just want to get out of the flesh.' 'What makes you feel so joyful?' 'Well, I don't know.' Should we not think such a person unreasonable?

There are a great many people who want to feel that they are Christians, before they are Christians; they want the Christian's experience, before they become Christians; they want to have the joy of the Lord, before they receive Jesus Christ. But this is not the Gospel order. He brings joy when He comes, and we cannot have joy apart from Him. There is no joy away from Him; He is the Author of it, and we find our joy in Him.

Joy is Unselfish

Now, there are three kinds of Joy; there is the joy of one's own salvation. I thought, when I first tasted that, it was the most delicious joy I had ever known, and that I could never get beyond it. But I found afterwards, there was something more joyful than that, namely, the joy of the salvation of others. Oh, the privilege, the blessed privilege, to be used of God to win a soul to Christ; and to see a man or woman being led out of bondage by some act of ours toward them, or some word of ours spoken to them! To think that God should condescend to allow us to be co-workers with Him. It is the highest honour we can wear. This joy of seeing others saved surpasses even the joy of our own salvation. And then John said, he had no greater joy than to see his disciples walking in the truth (3 John 4). Every man who has been the means of leading souls to Christ understands what that means. Young disciples, walk in the truth, and you will have joy all the while!

I think there is a difference between Happiness and Joy. Happiness is caused by things which happen around me; and circumstances will mar it: but joy flows right on through trouble; joy flows on through the dark; joy flows in the night as well as in the day; joy flows all through persecution and opposition: it flows right along, for it is an unceasing fountain bubbling up in the heart; a secret spring which the world cannot see, and knows nothing about – the Lord gives His people perpetual joy when they walk in obedience to Him.

This joy is fed by the Divine Word. Jeremiah says (15:16):

> *'Thy words were found, and I did eat them; and Thy Word was unto me the joy and rejoicing of mine heart; for I am called by Thy name, O Lord God of hosts.'*

He ate the words; and what was the result? He said they were the joy and rejoicing of his heart. Now people should look for joy in the Word, and not in the world: they should look for the joy which the Scriptures furnish, and then go and work in the vineyard; because a joy that does not send me out to someone else, a joy that does not impel me to go and help the poor drunkard, a joy that does not prompt me to visit the widow and the fatherless, a joy that does not cause me to go into the Mission Sunday-school or other Christian work, is not worth having, and is not from above; a joy that does not constrain me to go and work for the Master, is purely sentiment, and not real joy.

Joy in Persecution

Then we read in Luke 6:22 and 23:

> *'Blessed are ye, when men shall hate you, and when they shall separate you from their company, and shall reproach you, and cast out your name as evil, for the Son of Man's sake. Rejoice ye in that day, and leap for joy; for behold, your reward is great in heaven; for in the like manner did their fathers unto the prophets.'*

Christians do not receive their reward down here. We have to go right against the current of the world. We may be unpopular; and we may have to go right against many of our personal friends, if we live godly in Christ Jesus. At the same time, if we are persecuted for the Master's sake, we shall have this joy bubbling up; it just comes right up in our hearts all the while – a joy that is unceasing – that flows right on. The world cannot choke that fountain.

If we have Christ in the heart, by-and-by the reward will come. The longer I live the more I am convinced that godly men and women are not appreciated in our day. But their work will live after them; and there will probably be a greater work done after they are gone, by the influence of their lives, than when they were living. Daniel is doing a thousand times more now, than when he was living in Babylon. Abraham is doing more to-day than he did on the plain with his tent and altar: all these centuries he has been living. And so we read,

> *'Blessed are the dead which die in the Lord, from hence-forth: yea, saith the Spirit, that they may rest from their labours; and their works do follow them.'*

(Revelation 14:13)

Let us set the streams running that shall flow on after we have gone. If we have to-day persecution and opposition, let us press forward, and our reward will be great by-and-by. Oh, think of this; the Lord Jesus, the Maker of heaven and earth, who created the world, says, *'Great shall be thy reward.'* He calls it great. If some friend should say it was great, it might prove very small; but when the Lord, the great and mighty God, says it is great, what must it be! Oh, the reward that is in store for those who serve Him! We have this joy, if we serve Him.

A man or woman who is cast down, is not fit to work for God, because such a one goes about the work with a tell-tale face. *'The joy of the Lord is your strength.'* What we need to-day is a joyful church. A joyful church will make inroads upon the works of Satan; and we shall see the Gospel going down into dark lanes and dark alleys, and into dark garrets and cellars; and we shall see the drunkards reached, and the gamblers and the harlots come pressing into the kingdom of God. It is this carrying a sad countenance, with so many wrinkles on our brows, that retards Christianity. Oh, may there come great joy upon believers everywhere, so that we may shout for joy, and rejoice in God day and night! A joyful church – let us pray for this, that the Lord may make us joyful; and when we have joy, then we shall have success: and if here we do not find the reward we think we ought to have, let us constantly remember the time for reward will come hereafter.

Someone has said, if you had asked men in Abraham's day who their greatest man was, they would have said Enoch, and not Abraham. If you had asked in Moses' day who their greatest man was, they would not have said it was Moses; he would have been nothing: but it would have been Abraham. If you had asked in the days of Elijah or Daniel, it would not have been Daniel or Elijah; they were nothing: but it would have been Moses. And if you had asked in the days of Jesus Christ about John the Baptist or the apostles, you would have heard they were mean and contemptible in the sight of the world, and were looked upon with scorn and reproach. But see how mighty they have become! And so we shall not be appreciated in our day; but we are to toil on and work on, possessing this joy all the while. And if we lack it, let us cry:

> *'Restore unto me the joy of Thy salvation, and uphold me with Thy free Spirit; then will I teach transgressors Thy ways, and sinners shall be converted unto Thee.'*
>
> (Psalm 51:12, 13)

Again, it is written, John 15:11:

> *'These things have I spoken unto you, that My joy might remain in you, and that your joy might be full.'*

And in 16:22:

> *'And ye now therefore have sorrow; but I will see you again, and your heart shall rejoice, and your joy no man taketh from you.'*

I am so thankful that I have a joy that the world cannot rob me of. I have a treasure that the world cannot take from me; I have something that it is not in the power of man or devil to deprive me of; and that is the joy of the Lord. *'No man taketh it from you'* (John 16:22). In the second century, they brought a martyr before a king, and the king wanted him to recant and give up Christ and Christianity; but the man spurned the proposition. But the king said: 'If you do not do it, I shall banish you.' The man smiled, and answered: 'You cannot banish me from Christ; for He says He will never leave me nor forsake me.' The king became angry, and said: 'Well, I will confiscate your property, and take it all from you.' And the man replied: 'My treasures are laid up on high; you cannot get them.' The king became still more angry, and said: 'I will kill you.' 'Why,' the man answered, 'I have been dead forty years: I have been dead with Christ; dead to the world: my life is hid with Christ in God; and you cannot touch it.'

And so we can rejoice, because we are on resurrection

ground, having risen with Christ. Let persecution and opposition come! – we can rejoice continually. And remember – that our reward is great, reserved for us unto the day when He who is our Life shall appear, and we also shall appear with Him in glory.

∽ ∾

'The strokes of the "sword of the Spirit" alight only on the conscience; and its edge is anointed with a balm to heal every wound it may inflict.'
Dr J. Harris

'Every vain thought and idle word, and every wicked deed, are like so many drops to quench the Spirit of God. Some quench Him with the lust of the flesh; some quench Him with cares of the mind; some quench Him with long delays – that is, not plying the motion when it cometh, but crossing the good thoughts with bad thoughts, and doing a thing when the Spirit saith not. The Spirit is often grieved, before He be quenched.'
H. Smith

'In times when vile men held the high places of the land, a roll of drums was employed to drown the martyr's voice, lest the testimony of truth from the scaffold should reach the ears of the people – an illustration of how men deal with their own consciences, and seek to put to silence the truth-telling voice of the Holy Spirit.'
Arnot

∽ ∾

Chapter 5

Power Hindered

Israel, we are told, limited the Holy One of Israel: they vexed and grieved the Holy Spirit, and rebelled against His authority (Psalm 78:41; Isaiah 63:10). But there is a special sin against Him, which we may profitably consider. The first description of it is in Matthew 12:22–32:

The Unpardonable Sin

'Then was brought unto Him one possessed with a devil, blind and dumb; and He healed him, insomuch that the blind and dumb both spake and saw. And all the people were amazed, and said, Is not this the Son of David?

'But when the Pharisees heard it, they said, This fellow doth not cast out devils, but by Beelzebub, the prince of the devils.

'And Jesus knew their thoughts, and said unto them, Every kingdom divided against itself is brought to desolation; and every city or house divided against itself shall not stand. And if Satan cast out Satan, he is divided against himself; how then shall his kingdom stand? And if I by Beelzebub cast out devils, by whom do your children cast them out? therefore they shall be your judges. But if I cast out devils by the Spirit of God, then the kingdom of God is come unto you. Or else how can one enter into a strong man's house, and spoil his goods, except he first bind the strong man? and then he will spoil his house.

'He that is not with Me is against Me; and he that gathereth not with Me, scattereth abroad. Wherefore I say unto you, All manner of sin and blasphemy shall be forgiven unto men; but the blasphemy against the Holy Ghost shall not be forgiven unto men. And whosoever speaketh a word against the Son of Man, it shall be forgiven him; but whosoever speaketh against the Holy Ghost, it shall not be forgiven him, neither in this world, neither in the world to come.'

That is Matthew's account. Now let us read Mark's account in chapter 3:21–29:

'And when His friends heard of it, they went out to lay hold on Him; for they said: He (that is Christ) *is beside Himself. And the scribes which came down from Jerusalem said, He hath Beelzebub; and by the prince of the devils casteth He out devils.'*

The word Beelzebub is said to mean *'the Lord of Filth.'* These scribes charged the Lord Jesus with being possessed not only with an evil spirit, but with a filthy spirit.

'And He called them unto Him, and said unto them in parables, How can Satan cast out Satan? And if a kingdom be divided against itself, that kingdom cannot stand. And if a house be divided against itself, that house cannot stand. And if Satan rise up against himself, and be divided, he cannot stand, but hath an end. No man can enter into a strong man's house, and spoil his goods, except he will first bind the strong man, and then he will spoil his house. Verily I say unto you, All sins shall be forgiven unto the sons of men, and blasphemies wherewith soever they shall blaspheme: but he that shall blaspheme against the Holy Ghost hath never forgiveness, but is in danger of eternal damnation.'

Now, if it stopped there, we should perhaps be left in darkness, and should not exactly understand what the sin against the Holy Ghost is. But the next verse of this same chapter of Mark just throws light upon the whole matter: and we need not be in darkness another minute if we really want light; for observe, the verse reads: *'Because they said, He hath an unclean spirit.'*

Now, I have met a good many atheists and sceptics, deists and infidels, both in this country and abroad; but I never in my life met a man or woman who said that Jesus Christ was possessed of an unclean devil. Did you? I do not think you ever met such a person. I have heard men say bitter things against Christ; but I never heard any man stand up and say that he thought Jesus Christ was possessed with the devil, or that He cast out devils by the power of the devil; and I do not believe any man or woman has any right to say they have committed the unpardonable sin, unless they have maliciously, and wilfully, and deliberately, said that they believe that Jesus Christ had a devil in Him; and that He was under the power of the devil; and that He cast out devils by the power of the devil. Because you, perhaps, have heard someone say that there is such a thing as grieving the Spirit of God, and resisting the Spirit of God until He has taken His flight and left you, you have said, 'That is the unpardonable sin.'

What It Is Not

I admit there is such a thing as RESISTING the Spirit of God, and resisting till the Spirit of God has departed, but if the Spirit of God has left any, they will not be troubled about their sins. The very fact that men are troubled, shows that the Spirit of God has not left them. If a man is troubled about his sins, it is the work of the Spirit; for Satan never yet told a man he was a sinner. Satan makes us believe that we are pretty good; that we are good enough without God, safe without Christ, and that we do not need salvation. But when a man wakes up to the fact that he is lost, that he is a sinner, *that* is the work of the Spirit; if the Spirit of God had left him he would not be in that state: the very fact that any men and women want to be Christians, is a sign that the Spirit of God is drawing them.

If resisting the Spirit of God is the unpardonable sin, then we have all committed it, and there is no hope for any of us; for I do not believe there is a minister, or a worker in Christ's vineyard, who has not, some time in his life, resisted the Holy Ghost; who has not, some time in his life, rejected the Spirit of God. To resist the Holy Ghost is one thing, and to commit that awful sin of *'blasphemy against the Holy Ghost'* (Matthew 12:31) is another thing; and we want to take the Scripture and just compare these two things. Now, some people say, 'I have such blasphemous thoughts; there are some awful thoughts that come into my mind against God;' and they think that is the unpardonable sin. We are not to blame for having

Bad Thoughts

come into our minds. If we harbour them, then we are to blame. But if the devil comes and darts an evil thought into my mind, and I say, 'Lord, help me!' sin is not reckoned to me. Who has not had evil thoughts come into his mind, flash into his heart, and been called to fight them!

One old divine says, 'You are not to blame for the birds that fly over your head; but if you allow them to come down and make a nest in your hair, then you are to blame. You are to blame if you do not fight them off.' And so with these evil thoughts that come flashing into our minds; we have to fight them; we are not to harbour them; we are not to entertain them. If I have evil thoughts and evil desires come into my mind, it is no sign that I have committed the unpardonable sin. If I love these thoughts and harbour them, and think evil of God, and think Jesus Christ is a blasphemer, I am responsible for such gross iniquity; but if I charge Him with being the prince of devils, then I am committing the unpardonable sin.

The Faithful Friend

Let us now consider the sin of **Grieving** the Spirit. *Resisting* the Holy Ghost is one thing; *grieving* Him is another. Stephen charged the unbelieving Jews in Acts 7:51, *'Ye do always* *resist the Holy Ghost; as your fathers did, so do ye.'* The world in all ages has been resisting the Spirit of God. That is the history of the world. The world is to-day resisting the Holy Spirit.

'Faithful are the wounds of a friend' (Proverbs 27:6). The Divine Spirit, as a Friend, reveals to this poor world its faults; and the world only hates Him for it. He shows men the plague of their hearts. He convinces or convicts them of sin; therefore they fight the Spirit of God. I believe there is many a man resisting the Holy Ghost; I believe there is many a man to-day fighting against the Spirit of God.

In Ephesians 4:30–32, we read:

> *'Grieve not the Holy Spirit of God, whereby ye are sealed unto the day of redemption. Let all bitterness, and wrath, and anger, and clamour, and evil speaking, be put away from you, with all malice: and be ye kind one to another, tender-hearted, forgiving one another; even as God for Christ's sake hath forgiven you.'*

Now, mark you, that was written to the Church at Ephesus. *'Grieve not the Holy Spirit, whereby ye are sealed unto the day of redemption.'* I believe to-day the Church all over Christendom is guilty of grieving the Holy Spirit.

There are a good many believers in different churches wondering why the work of God is not revived.

Grieve Not the Spirit!

I think that if we search, we shall find something in the Church grieving the Spirit of God: it may be a mere schism in the church; it may be some unsound doctrine; it may be some division in the Church. There is one thing I have noticed as I have travelled in different countries: I have never yet known the Spirit of God work where the Lord's people were divided. If we are to have the Holy Spirit of God to work in our midst, there is one thing that we must have; and that is unity. If a church is divided, the members should immediately seek unity. Let the believers come together, and get the difficulty out of the way. If the minister of a church cannot unite the people – if those who are dissatisfied will not fall in – it will be better for that minister to retire.

I think there are a good many ministers both in England and America who are losing their time: they have lost, some of them, months and years; they have not seen any fruit, and they will not see any fruit, because they have a divided church. Such a church cannot grow in divine things. The Spirit of God does not work where there is division. What we want to-day is the spirit of unity amongst God's children, so that the Lord may work.

Worldly Amusements

Then, another thing, I think, that grieves the Spirit, is the miserable policy of introducing questionable entertainments. There are the lotteries, for instance, that we have in many churches. If a man wants to gamble, he has not to go to some gambling den; he can stay in the church. And there are fairs – bazaars, as they call them – where they have rafflings and grab-bags. And if a man wants to see a drama, he does not need to go to the theatre, for many of the churches are turned into theatres; he may stay right in the church and witness the acting. I believe all these things grieve the Spirit of God. I believe when we bring the Church down to the level of the world to reach the world, we are all the while grieving and losing the Spirit of God.

Unconverted Choirs

But some say, 'If we take that standard and lift it up high, it will drive away a great many members from our churches.' I believe it. And I think the quicker they are gone the better. The world has come into the Church like a flood. How often you find an unconverted choir employed to do the singing for the whole congregation! The idea that we need an ungodly man to sing praises to God! It was not long ago I heard of a church where they had an unconverted choir, and the minister saw something about the choir that he did not like; he spoke to the chorister, but the chorister replied: 'You attend to your end of the church, and I will attend to mine.' You cannot expect the Spirit of God to work in a church in such a state as that.

In the first Epistle to the Corinthians Paul, speaking of unknown tongues, says,

> *'If I know not the meaning of the voice I shall be unto him that speaketh a barbarian; and he that speaketh shall be a barbarian unto me.'*   (1 Corinthians 14:11)

And if we have choirs who are singing in an unknown tongue, is not that just as barbarous? I have been in churches where they have had a choir, who would rise and sing five or ten minutes, and I could not understand one solitary word they sang; and all the while the people were looking around carelessly.

There are, perhaps, a select few, very fond of fine music; and they want to bring the opera right into the church: and so they have opera music in the church; and the people, who are drowsy and sleepy, take no part in the singing. They hire ungodly men, unconverted men; and these men will sometimes get the Sunday papers, and get back in the organ loft, and the moment the minister begins his sermon, they will take out their newspapers and read them, while the minister is preaching. The organist, provided he does not go out for a walk – if he happen to keep awake, will read his paper, or, perhaps, a novel, while the minister is preaching; and the minister wonders why God does not revive his work; he wonders why he is losing his hold on the congregation; he wonders why people do not come crowding into the church – why people are running after the world instead of coming into church. The trouble is that we have let down the standard; we have grieved the Spirit of God. One movement of God's power is worth more than all our artificial power; and what the Church of God wants to-day is to get down in the dust of humiliation and confession of sin, and come out and be separate from the world. And then see if we do not have power with God and with man.

What is Success?

The Gospel has not lost its power; it is just as powerful to-day as it ever has been. We want no new doctrine. It is still the old Gospel with the old power, the Holy Ghost power; and if the churches will but confess their sins and put them away; if they will but lift up the standard higher instead of pulling it down, and pray to God to raise us all up into a higher and holier life, then the fear of the Lord will come upon the people around us.

When Jacob set his face toward Bethel and put away strange gods, the terror of God fell upon the cities round about them (Genesis 35:5). And when the churches turn toward God, and we cease grieving the Spirit, so that He may work through us, we shall then have conversions all the while. Believers will be added to the Church daily. It is sad when you look over Christendom and see how desolate it is, and note how little spiritual life, how little spiritual power, there is in the Church of God to-day. Many of the church members do not even want this Holy Ghost power. They do not desire it; they want intellectual power; they want to get some man who will 'draw', and a choir that will 'draw'; not caring whether anyone is saved. With them *that* is not the question – only to fill the pews, have good society, fashionable people, and dancing. Such persons are found one night at the theatre and the next night at the opera. They do not like the prayer-meetings; they abominate them: if the minister will only lecture and entertain, that will suit them. I said to a man some time ago, 'How are you getting on at your church?' 'Oh, splendid.' 'Many conversions?' 'Well – well, on that side we are not getting on so well: but,' he said, 'we have let all our pews, and are able to pay all our running expenses; we are getting on splendidly.' That is what the godless call getting on 'splendidly'; because they let the pews, pay the minister, and meet all the running expenses. Conversion! that is a 'strange thing'.

There was a man being shown through one of the cathedrals of Europe; he had come from the country, and one of the men belonging to the cathedral was showing him round, when he inquired, 'Do you have many conversions here?' 'Many what?' 'Many conversions here?' 'Ah, man, this is not a Wesleyan chapel.' The idea of there being conversions there! You can go into a good many churches both in England and America, and ask if they have many conversions there, and they would not know what you meant, they are so far away from the Lord; they are not looking for conversions, and do not expect them.

Shipwrecks

Alas, how many young converts have made shipwreck against such churches! Instead of being a harbour of safety to them, they have held out false lights, luring them to destruction. Is it not time for us to get down on our knees before God, and cry mightily to Him to forgive us our sins? The quicker we own them the better. You may be invited to a party, and it may be made up of church members. And what will be the conversation? Oh, I got so sick of such parties that I gave them up years ago; I should not think of spending an evening that way; it is a waste of time: there is hardly a chance to say a word for the Master. If you talk of a personal Christ, your company becomes offensive; people do not like it: they want you to talk about the world, about a popular minister, a popular church, a good organ, a good choir; and they say, 'Oh, we have a grand organ, and a superb choir,' and all that; and it suits them: but that does not warm the Christian heart. When you speak of a risen Christ and a personal Saviour, they do not like it. The fact is, the world has come into the church and taken possession of it; and what we need to do is to wake up, and ask God to forgive us for 'grieving the Spirit.'

Dear reader, search your heart and inquire, Have I done anything to grieve the Spirit of God? If you have, may God show it you to-day! If you have done anything to grieve the Spirit of God, you need to know it to-day, and to get down on your knees before God, and ask Him to forgive you and help you to put it away. I have lived long enough to feel that if I cannot have the power of the Spirit of God upon me to help me to work for the Lord, I would rather die: yes, I would rather die, than live just for the sake of living. How many are there in the church to-day, who have been members for fifteen or twenty years, but have never done a solitary thing for Jesus Christ! They cannot lay their hands upon one solitary soul who has been blessed through their influence; they cannot point to-day to one single person who has ever been lifted up by them.

Quench not the Spirit

In 1st Thessalonians (5:19), we are thus exhorted: *'Quench not the Spirit.'* Now, I am confident the cares of the world are coming in, and quenching the Spirit with a great many. They say: 'I don't care for the world:' – perhaps, after all, it is not so much the *pleasures* of the world as the *cares* of this life that are dragging them down; but they have just let the cares come in and quench the Spirit of God. Anything that comes between me and God – between my soul and God – quenches the Spirit. It may be my family. You may say: 'Is there any danger of my loving my family too much?' Not if we love God more; but God must have the first place. If I love my family more than God, then I am quenching the Spirit of God within me; if I love wealth, if I love fame, if I love honour, if I love position, if I love pleasure, if I love self, more than I love God who created and saved me, then I am committing a sin; I am not only grieving the Spirit of God, but quenching Him, and robbing my soul of His power.

Emblems of the Spirit

But I would further call attention to the emblems of the Holy Spirit. An emblem is something that represents an object; just as a balance is an emblem of justice, and a crown an emblem of royalty, and a sceptre an emblem of power. We find in Exodus 17:6, that water is an emblem of the Holy

Spirit. You find in the smitten rock in the wilderness the work of the Trinity illustrated.

> *'Behold, I will stand before thee there upon the rock in Horeb; and thou shalt smite the rock, and there shall come water out of it, that the people may drink. And Moses did so, in the sight of the elders of Israel.'*

Paul declares, in his Epistle to the Corinthians, that the rock was Christ (1 Corinthians 10:4); it represented Christ. God said: *'I will stand upon the rock;'* and as Moses smote the rock the water flowed out. That water was an emblem of the Holy Spirit; and it flowed out along through the camp; and the people drank of the water. Now **Water** is cleansing; it is fertilizing; it is refreshing; it is abundant; and it is freely given: and so the Spirit of God is the same – cleansing, fertilizing, refreshing, reviving; and He was freely given when the smitten Christ was glorified.

Then, too, **Fire** is an emblem of the Spirit; it is purifying, illuminating, searching. We talk about searching our hearts. We cannot do it. What we want is to have God search them. Oh that God may search us, and bring out the hidden things, the secret things, that cluster there; and bring them to light!

The **Wind** is another emblem. It is independent, powerful, sensible in its effects, and reviving. How the Spirit of God revives when He comes to the drooping members of the Church! Then the **Rain** and the **Dew** are emblems of the Spirit – fertilizing, refreshing, abundant. And the **Dove**, gentle – what more gentle than the dove? And the **Lamb** – meek, innocent, a sacrifice, is an emblem of Jesus. We read of the wrath of God; we read of the wrath of the Lamb; but nowhere do we read of the wrath of the Holy Spirit: He is gentle, innocent, meek, loving. And that Spirit wants to take possession of our hearts. And He comes as a **Voice**, another emblem – speaking, guiding, warning, teaching; and the **Seal** – impressing, securing, and making us His own.

May we know Him in all His wealth of blessing. This is my prayer for myself – for you. May we heed the words of the grand Apostle:

*'My speech and my preaching was not with enticing words of man's wisdom, but in demonstration of the Spirit, and of power: that your faith should not stand in the wisdom of men, **but in the power of God.**'*

(1 Corinthians 2:4, 5)